Practical Reality

JONATHAN DANCY

OXFORD
UNIVERSITY PRESS

OXFORD
UNIVERSITY PRESS

Great Clarendon Street, Oxford OX2 6DP

Oxford University Press is a department of the University of Oxford.
It furthers the University's objective of excellence in research, scholarship,
and education by publishing worldwide in

Oxford New York

Athens Auckland Bangkok Bogotá Buenos Aires Calcutta
Cape Town Chennai Dar es Salaam Delhi Florence Hong Kong Istanbul
Karachi Kuala Lumpur Madrid Melbourne Mexico City Mumbai
Nairobi Paris São Paulo Singapore Taipei Tokyo Toronto Warsaw

and associated companies in Berlin Ibadan

Published in the United States
by Oxford University Press Inc., New York

©Jonathan Dancy 2000

The moral rights of the author have been asserted
Database right Oxford University Press (maker)

First published 2000

British Library Cataloguing in Publication Data

Data available

Library of Congress Cataloging in Publication Data

Data available

ISBN 0-19-824115-1

1 3 5 7 9 10 8 6 4 2

Typeset by Best-set Typesetter Ltd., Hong Kong
Printed in Great Britain
on acid-free paper by
T.J. International Ltd
Padstow, Cornwall

à mes amis de Mordagne

PREFACE

This book brings together two large and distinct areas of enquiry. The first is the nature of good reasons for action, where we ask what it is for something to give us a reason to act in one way rather than another. The second is that part of the theory of action that asks what it is to act for a reason. It would not be quite correct to say that what is being offered here is a combination of value theory and the theory of motivation, for value theory is distinct from the theory of reasons. But there are views on which the distinction between values and reasons becomes pretty slight, and the view presented here is one (but only one) of those.

In broad outline, the first part of the book makes claims about the nature of practical reasons, those reasons that favour one action rather than another. The second part uses those claims to support an unfamiliar account of what it is to act for a reason, and to undermine more standard accounts.

The discussion is conducted at a fairly high level of abstraction, with few of the sort of examples that discuss the doings of Peter, Jane, and John that one often finds in contemporary philosophical writing. This has given me one problem. I speak constantly of the agent's reasons, of things that are reasons for an agent, and of reasons why the agent acted. As a result, I have been forced to choose between two practices. The first is that of allotting this abstract but omnipresent agent a gender and sticking to it; the second is that of varying the gender from case to case, in hopes of doing so arbitrarily. The second option, when I tried it, seemed to me to be just confusing and artificial, creating two abstract agents in the mind of the reader when it would be better to have only one. So I decided to think of this agent as effectively an abstract representation of myself, and as a result it—now he—is of the male gender throughout. To those whom this irritates, or worse, I apologize. I suppose I am hoping that after about twenty years of variable genders it might be possible for all authors now to write in terms of their own gender, without raising hackles.

ACKNOWLEDGEMENTS

I owe thanks first to All Souls College, Oxford, for a visiting fellowship which I held in 1993–4 and in which I began to work on the topic of this book: to the British Academy for a grant towards an extra term's research leave in autumn 1997, in which I wrote a first draft; and to the Research School of Social Science at the Australian National University for a visiting fellowship in early 1998, in which the first draft changed shape dramatically, in ideal academic conditions. Rüdiger Bittner, Arthur Collins, David McNaughton, and Fred Stoutland were kind enough to read the whole book in one form or another and send me detailed comments, which in each case led to significant improvements. I am grateful to David Bakhurst, who urged me to try to make things less complicated, and to Derek Parfit, who made me take the logic out or at least relegate it to an appendix. I owe much to the comments and constructive criticisms of the four anonymous referees who advised Oxford University Press about this book. And I owe thanks for their help and sometimes even encouragement to Lars Bergström, Bruno Celano, Roger Crisp, Peter Hacker, Govert den Hartog, John Heil, Richard Holton, Brad Hooker, Christopher Hookway, Keith Horton, Lloyd Humberstone, John Hyman, Frank Jackson, Maggie Little, Fraser McBride, Mike Martin, Ingmar Persson, Philip Pettit, Simon Prosser, Joseph Raz, Michael Smith, Rowland Stout, Philip Stratton-Lake, Bart Streumer, Chris Taylor, Candace Vogler, and Jay Wallace—and to audiences at places too numerous to mention.

J.D.
Reading
January 2000

CONTENTS

I

Reasons for Action

1. *Good Reasons and those for which the Agent Acted*

This enquiry begins from a perfectly ordinary and unproblematic distinction, expressed in terms of reasons. When someone does something, there will (normally) be some considerations in the light of which he acted—the reasons for which he did what he did. There are not so many things that we do for no reason at all. Intentional, deliberate, purposeful action is always done for a reason, even if some actions, such as recrossing one's legs, are not—or not always, anyway. So normally there will be, for each action, the reasons in the light of which the agent did that action, which we can think of as what persuaded him to do it. When we think in terms of reasons in this way, we think of them as *motivating*. The consideration that motivated the agent was his reason for doing what he did.

We may, of course, know the reasons for which the agent acted without yet knowing whether there was a good reason to do what he did. Was there, for instance, some moral reason for him to do it? Or was there a reason of another sort? Was it at least a sensible thing to do in the circumstances? If it was a sensible thing to do, there will be some reason why this was the case. When we think of such reasons, we think of features that speak in favour of the action (or against it). They are good reasons for doing the action. So they are *normative*, both in their own nature (they *favour* action, and they do it more or less strongly) and in their product, since they make actions right or wrong, sensible or unwise. When we think in terms of reasons in this way, we are thinking normatively. We could even call such a reason a *normative reason*. All such reasons are good reasons, though some will be much better than others. This is because a reason that favours an action must be a good one. A bad reason for doing something, if it is not merely a not very good reason for doing it, can only be no reason at all for doing it; if so, it is not a reason in the sense intended, since it does not favour the relevant action.

The distinction with which I have started is not particularly obscure or complicated. There are these two ways of using the notion of a reason *for* action, which address different questions. There is the question what were the considerations in the light of which, or despite which, he acted as he did. This issue about *his reasons for doing it* is a matter of motivation. There is also the question whether there was good reason to act in that way, as we say, *any reason for doing it* at all, one perhaps that made it sensible in the circumstances, morally required, or in some other way to be recommended, or whether there was more reason not to do it. (There are other reasons besides those that make actions right or sensible; there might be an aesthetic reason in favour of acting gracefully.) This second question raises a normative issue.

Because there are different questions at issue, the answers to them can differ. The consideration in the light of which someone acted as he did need not have been a very good reason; what he did may have been a pretty silly thing to do, with little or nothing actually to be said in its favour. In such a situation we can give his reasons for acting, and in that sense explain his action, but cannot find much to say in favour of what he did. Motivating reasons are supposed to be the ones that actually made a difference to how he acted; they constitute the light in which he chose to do what he did. Normative reasons are the ones we try to cite in favour of an action, because they are the ones that should show that the action was sensible or right or whatever. So if an agent does something extremely silly, we might say he had a motivating reason for doing what he did but little normative reason. What this means is that we can give a certain sort of explanation for his acting as he did, but we cannot defend it.

If we do speak in this way, of motivating and normative reasons, this should not be taken to suggest that there are two sorts of reason, the sort that motivate and the sort that are good. There are not. There are just two questions that we use the single notion of a reason to answer. When I call a reason 'motivating', all that I am doing is issuing a reminder that the focus of our attention is on matters of motivation, for the moment. When I call it 'normative', again all that I am doing is stressing that we are currently thinking about whether it is a good reason, one that favours acting in the way proposed.

If an agent does a truly bad or silly action, then, he will surely have acted for some reason; he will, that is, have had a motivating reason for doing what he did. But there will have been little reason to act in that way. In the worst possible case, indeed, we would have to say that there was no reason at all for doing what he did (no good reason, that is). This would happen if the features that the agent took to count in favour of acting in fact do nothing of the sort; this might happen when making complicated financial decisions, for instance, for one can easily get confused in such cases and make a complete mistake about which way a consideration counts. Things are not often quite as bad as this, of course. In the best case, there is some good reason for doing the action, and the reason that motivates the agent coincides with that reason. In another case, there may be a wealth of good reasons present, with only some of these actually doing the motivating, i.e. functioning as the agent's reason for action. In yet another, there may be perfectly good reasons for doing it, though actually what motivated the agent was something quite different. In all these cases, we might say, there is some defence for the agent acting as he did, or at least for what was done, even if not for the way he did it.

On the other hand, there may be very good reasons favouring an action though these influence the agent not at all, either because he is simply ignorant of them, or because, though perfectly well aware of them, he is lazy, selfish, pig-headed, or whatever. If so, the action, though there are good reasons to do it, will just not get done. None of those reasons motivated the agent to do this sensible thing. He went off and did something else, without a second thought.

The main awkwardness of what we have so far is that it leaves us saying that an agent can act for a reason (a motivating one) that is no reason (no good reason, that is), or that there was no reason to do what he did, even though he did it for a reason. Some motivating reasons, that is, are not good reasons. But I take this to be no more than a little local difficulty. It seems awkward because the phrase 'good reason' is pleonastic, when we are thinking normatively, and this leads us to say that a motivating reason that is no good reason is not a reason either. But we should remember that the notion of a reason is used to answer two distinct questions. The first is why someone acted, and the second is the pleonastic one of

whether there were any (good) reasons for so acting. In specifying
an agent's motivating reasons we answer the first question, and *in
that sense* motivating reasons are all reasons. It is only when we
have our eyes on the second question that we want to allow that a
motivating reason can be no reason at all. In what follows, the
phrase 'good reason' will be a mark that we are thinking in normative terms.

   In laying out the distinction between good reasons and those that
motivate, I have spoken as if, when we act, the reasons that motivate us are all on the side of doing what we did. I have given the
impression that the considerations in the light of which we act all
pull us in the direction of doing the action, with none tugging
unsuccessfully in the other direction. But in fact there can be considerations despite which we acted, considerations that would have
led us not to do it if they could have done (if, for instance, there
had been fewer considerations pulling in the other direction), and
so on. I might decide to buy that new book even though it is very
expensive. Here we have a consideration pulling against the action
that I choose to do, but pulling unsuccessfully. I recognize it as a
reason, and am influenced by it, but not enough to stop me from
acting. As we might say, 'I was moved by her plight, but not enough
to do anything about it'. What is more, as well as reasons that pull
directly against doing the action, I might recognize reasons for
doing each of two things, when I cannot do both at once. This
weekend I am motivated both to dig over the vegetable patch and
to overhaul my bicycle, but I have not the time to do both. Suppose
I decide to deal with the bicycle and leave the garden until later.
Are my defeated motivators to be thought of as among the reasons
that motivated me? They are not among my reasons for doing what
I did. In that sense, then, they are not among the reasons that motivated me to act. Thinking in relation to the action that was done,
then, they do not count among the motivating reasons. But still I
was influenced by them, and they do figure in my motivational
economy. We should not forget this, but all the same I will normally
speak as if the reasons that do motivate all pull in the same direction. This should not blind us to the fact that not all such reasons
actually succeed in getting one to act.

   There is a similar issue about whether all good reasons lie on the
same side, or whether there can be good reasons on both sides of
the question. But it is easier to take a firm stance on this one. There

can be good reasons not to do an action even when there are better reasons to do it. That an action was right does not show that there were no (good) reasons not to do it. Equally, if an action was wrong, this does not mean that there was no reason to do it; it merely means that there was insufficient reason.

2. *The Reason Why*

We can normally explain an agent's doing what he did by specifying the reasons in the light of which he acted. But there are other ways of explaining an action—ways that do not involve specifying the agent's reason (Darwall 1983: 29). For instance, we might say that the reason why he did this was that he had forgotten his promise to her. In so explaining his action, we are not involved in laying out the reasons in the light of which he acted. We are not supposing that the considerations that he took to favour the action included that he had forgotten his promise to her. When we mention the fact that he had forgotten his promise, we mention something of which he was wholly unconscious, and which could not have been among his reasons for acting. This is quite apart from the fact that one's having forgotten something is not normally able to be taken even by others as a reason in favour of doing what one did, though of course it can be some excuse.

On other occasions we explain an action by appeal to quite different sorts of consideration. What explains why one person yawned may be that someone else yawned just next to them. What explains why he responded so aggressively may be that he is having trouble at home or that he has taken a particular form of medication. What explains why he gave this student a better grade than she deserved is that he was unconsciously influenced by the fact that she always dresses so neatly (or something even less defensible). What explains why so many people buy expensive perfume at Christmas is the barrage of advertising on the television. What explains why he didn't come to the party is that he is shy. In none of these cases are we specifying considerations in the light of which these things were done. But in all of them we are explaining why they were done. It seems, therefore, as if there is a wide range of things we think of as capable of giving answers to the question 'Why did he do that?' These answers range from specifying the things in the light of which the agent chose to do what he did, which we have sometimes called the agent's reasons for doing what he did, to something that is not a reason at all, really, but rather a cause (as in the explanation that talks about medication).

So we need to keep the notion of a motivating reason separate in our minds from the more general notion of 'the reason why the agent did what he did'. In what follows, the phrase 'in the light of' will be used to signify the relation between an agent and the reasons for which the agent acted. And I will speak of the agent's reasons in a similar way. The agent's reasons are the reasons that motivated him, namely the considerations in the light of which he chose to do what he did. But not all explanations of action specify motivating reasons in this sense.

3. *Other Versions of the Motivating–Normative Distinction*

I have characterized the distinction between the reasons why we do things and the reasons in favour of doing them in terms of the motivating and the normative. In doing so, I have tried to avoid any suggestion that we are dealing here with two sorts of reason. This is because the main argument of this book is that one and the same reason can be both motivating and normative. A reason for acting can be the reason why one acted. This should not look very surprising, one would have thought—until one notices that most contemporary philosophers take it to be impossible. All this will emerge in Chapter 5.

The terms 'motivating' and 'normative', though perfectly standard in the literature, are not the ones that everyone uses. Some writers speak of justifying rather than normative reasons; others— sometimes the same ones—speak of explanatory rather than motivating reasons. The distinction intended is, I think, the same all the time. I give here some defence of my preference for the terms I have adopted.

Talking of justifying reasons rather than normative or good ones runs foul of one difficulty that I hope to be able to keep under control. This is that agents may do things that are actually ill-advised, but be able to explain why they did these things in such a way as to defend their choice of action, without this showing that what they did was in fact the sensible thing to do. Suppose, for instance, I make a not very sensible choice about what arrangements to make about my pension. And suppose that I can later explain the choice I made by pointing out that there were some crucial facts that I happened quite reasonably to have got wrong, and in this way, as we might put it, exculpate myself. There is a sense of 'justify' in which I can be said to have justified doing what I did. But this does not show that the balance of reasons was in favour of the action. It wasn't. Indeed, the features in the light of which I made my choice turned out all to be a mistake, and so cannot count even as defeated reasons. So I prefer to keep the notion of a reason that justifies separate from that of a normative reason. One might try to talk of a rectifying reason, one that shows the action that it supports to have been right, in preference to a justifying reason, one that defends the action without showing it to have been right. But this is too moralistic to be usable in every case.

Some writers speak of explanatory reasons rather than of motivating ones. My difficulty with this is that there is a sense in which normative reasons are explanatory; they explain why the action was right, or sensible, or whatever—why it was worth doing. What I have been calling 'reasons-why' will also be explanatory without being motivating, too, for I am thinking of motivating reasons only as considerations in the light of which the agent acted, and 'reasons-why' are not like that.

Some writers use phrases like 'the agent's normative reasons' (Smith 1994: 131). These appear to be a sort of hybrid. We might have thought that the reasons that motivated belong to the agent, as it were, and the normative ones are not particularly the agent's reasons at all; they are just the reasons why the action was to be recommended, the good reasons for doing it. What leads people to speak of the agent's normative reasons is that commonly (some would say universally) the reasons that motivate the agent are taken by the agent to be good reasons for doing what he did. It is because of this that they motivate the agent at all, we might say. When this happens, the reasons that motivate at least include what is here being called 'the agent's normative reasons'. I take it, however, that this phrase really refers to what the agent took to be good reasons, rather than to a special species of good reason, those somehow belonging to the agent. And that is how I will understand it in what follows.

4. *Justification and Explanation*

We have seen that there are (at least) two different sorts of question that we use the notion of a reason to answer. There are questions about why the agent did what he did, and questions about whether there was good reason to do it; there are reasons why people act, and reasons in favour of acting. Both questions are in a sense requests for explanation. The first sort of question asks for an explanation of the action that was done or is in prospect. The second sort of question asks for an account of whether the action is worth doing, which we give by giving the reasons that made it so, i.e. by explaining what made it so. But there is, it would seem, no one sort of request for explanation that both sorts of question address.

This has, however, been denied. Michael Smith has suggested that there is a broader sense in which, though there are indeed two questions, our answers to them are all aimed at the same thing. They are all attempts to render the relevant action intelligible, though there is more than one way of doing this, for we can render an action intelligible without explaining why it was done. Smith writes:

Motivating and normative reasons do have something in common in virtue of which they both count as reasons. For citing either would allow us to render an agent's action intelligible. This is essential. For there is an *a priori* connection between citing an agent's reasons for acting in a certain way and making her acting intelligible: that is, specifying what there is to be said for acting in the way in question. In virtue of their differences, however, motivating and normative reasons make actions intelligible for quite different reasons. (1994: 95)

Smith does not seem to tell us here what exactly the supposed a priori connection amounts to. But I presume that he has in mind the idea that to explain an action is to show how doing that action can have come to seem worth while to the agent. The action is explained once we can show that doing it made good sense in the lights of the agent. Now of course it is not required for this that we show that there was indeed good reason to do the action. For if it were, stupid and/or wrong actions would be inexplicable, which they are not. To explain them we show, not that they were sensible, but how it was that doing them appeared sensible to the agent. We lay out, as it were, the favourable light in which the action appeared to the agent.

This means that, to explain the action, we show how doing it can have made sense to the agent. And to do this we lay out the agent's take on things, and show that the action made sense in that light. So what we show is that, relative to how the agent took things to be, it made good sense to do this action. If things had been as he supposed, this action would indeed have been the right or the sensible thing to do.

There are two questions we can ask, then:

1. Did he do the right thing?
2. Had things been the way he supposed them to be, would what he did have been right?

The answer to the first question may be no even if the answer to the second is yes. Take a case where he (perhaps reasonably) believes that she would welcome his advances but is too shy to do much to encourage him. He acts in a way that would have been right if things had been as he supposed. But in fact things are not as he supposed, and what he does is not right (though perhaps pardonable, if his original belief was reasonable rather than, say, the result of lustful thinking).

Smith's remarks were not concerned only with moral reasons, but with practical reasons in general. And indeed we see that the distinction drawn above for the moral case can be drawn more generally, in terms of what there is most reason to do. There are two questions:

1. Did he do what there was most reason to do?
2. Had things been the way he supposed them to be, would his action have been the one there was most reason to do?

We explain the action by showing that the answer to the second question is yes. We make sense of the agent's doing what he did, even when there was inadequate reason to do it, by showing that he would have had good reason had things been as he supposed.

What this shows is that to explain an action is to justify it only in a certain sense. It is not to show that it was what there was most reason to do. It is to show that it would have been if the agent's beliefs had been true. But to show this much is to mount some defence of the agent for so acting. For the agent's behaviour is pardonable if (roughly) his beliefs were pardonable and had they been true he would have been doing what he ought, or what there was most reason to do.[1]

We can now see what lies behind Smith's remark that we make acting in a certain way intelligible by specifying what there is to be said for acting in that way. But to do so we have had to take the phrase 'what there is to be said for' as meaning rather 'what there seemed to be said for'. The link between explanation and justification is therefore a link between explaining the action and showing how, had things been as the agent supposed, there would have been most reason to do what he did.

5. *Four More Distinctions*

In this section I consider four further distinctions The first two of these concern motivation, the last one concerns the nature of good reasons, and the third concerns the relation between good reasons and motivation.

Humeanism and Anti-Humeanism in the Theory of Motivation

There is a classic position in the theory of motivation that is known as Humeanism, despite the fact that it bears little resemblance to the views of its supposed progenitor, David Hume. The basic claim made by this theory is that intentional actions are to be explained by reference to the beliefs and desires of the agent. For an intentional action to take place, its agent must have a suitable combination of beliefs and desires. There must be something that the agent wants, an aim or goal which the proposed action subserves in some way. It may do this as a means to an end, or in some other way, perhaps constitutively, as when taking care over my children's

---

[1] There are, in fact, two notions of a pardonable but false belief that we need to keep separate in our minds. There are beliefs that are unpardonable because they are beliefs that it is morally wrong to have; one should not, perhaps, believe that one is more morally significant than others are. This is an absolute notion of what is and is not pardonable. There are also beliefs that are pardonable given one's epistemic circumstances—the evidence available, for instance, or the time available for reflection. We could think of this as a relative notion of what is pardonable or unpardonable, since it is determined by considerations of what resources of various sorts were available to the agent.

education subserves my aim of being a good parent, not by being a means to that end but by being part of that end. Further, the agent must have suitable beliefs to the effect that the action is likely to subserve that goal. To take a very ordinary case, why is the agent walking towards that cupboard? He is doing this because he wants a glass of beer, and he believes that there is beer in the cupboard. So walking towards the cupboard subserves his aim of having a beer.

It is possible to object to Humeanism on the very simple grounds that we often do things that we do not want to do, either in themselves or as means to some end that we want to pursue or promote. Certainly, the ordinary use of the word 'desire' is restricted in a way that would render ridiculous any claim that all action is motivated by desire; its main use nowadays seems to be in sexual contexts. But when philosophers speak of desire, at least in the context of the theory of motivation, they are to some extent constructing a term of art. I may say that I am doing this because it is my duty, though I have no desire to do it whatever. The reply is that I must none the less take a positive attitude to some aspect of what I am doing—a 'pro-attitude', in current terms owed to W. D. Ross. And the current philosophical use of the term 'desire' takes it to be equivalent to this much broader notion of a pro-attitude. In this sense it becomes much more plausible to say that all action is motivated by desire.

Humeanism does not content itself with asserting the need for both beliefs and desires if there is to be intentional action. It also claims that the desire is in some way the dominant partner in the belief–desire combination. This point used to be made in terms of a hydraulic metaphor. If an agent is to change from rest to movement, there has to be some motive force that is capable of creating this change. Desire is such a force, being an active, urgent, pushy state. Belief, by contrast, is a static state, a passive, inert, or at least inactive conception of the situation. So the desire plays a role in the belief–desire combination that the belief is quite incapable of playing, and, as we might put it, it is the desire that makes the real difference. Desire can do nothing without belief, of course, since if we cannot attribute to the agent some suitable conception of the situation, we would be unable to explain the eventual action. For there would be no reason for the agent to do one thing rather than another, and so we would be unable to explain what he in fact did. Desire needs belief, then, as belief needs desire. But desire predominates.

If the sense in which desire predominates is not yet clear, that is a fair representation of the present state of Humean theory of motivation. Perhaps the nearest Humeans have got to making it clear is to ground talk about the predominance of desire in the distinction between two directions of fit. Belief has one direction of fit and desire has the other. A belief is out to fit the world, and if it fails to fit that world, the fault, as we might put it, lies with the belief rather than with the world. A desire is not shown to need revision if it fails to fit the world. Desire knows that things may not be (indeed probably are not) the way it represents them as to be, and is not to be criticized for this. Desire is out to get the world to fit it. So belief is not out to change things, but to catch them as they are, while desire is out to change things. In this sense, a Humean might say, desire is active in a way that belief is not, and it is in this sense of activity that we can think of the active partner as dominant.[2]

Anti-Humean arguments have tended to be of one of two forms. The first takes its cue from Thomas Nagel's distinction between motivated and motivating desire (Nagel 1970, ch. 5). Humeanism understands desire as leading, and as subserved by belief, and holds this conception in place by trying to think of desire as active in a way that belief is not. An opposing view, then, could argue that, though many actions are indeed to be explained in the Humean way, some are not. For some beliefs are capable themselves of generating the necessary desire, so that the belief is leading, dominant. The belief that the action would be unjust could cause in me a desire to have nothing to do with it, and the

---

[2] I have here suggested that a Humean might appeal to the notion of direction of fit to give sense to the idea that desire is active in a way that belief is not. This might be thought to be an admission that the very notion of a direction of fit can be used to support Humean claims about the dominance of desire in motivation. Worse, indeed, for I will shortly accept the distinction between two directions of fit, and may therefore be thought to commit myself to Humeanism, unwittingly. Not so, however. What I say in the text is that in virtue of its direction of fit, desire can be thought of as active in a way that belief is not. This admission, however, is perfectly compatible with the vigorously anti-Humean position I expound in Ch. 4. If, as I will there argue, desire cannot be part of what motivates, this imposes on us a non-Humean account of what motivates, but does not prevent desire (i.e. motivation) from being active in a way that belief is not. It does nothing to show that belief is not active in some other sense.

belief–desire combination thus formed would be what motivates me to abstain.

It is unclear from Nagel's own discussion whether this was the picture that he was trying to put up against the Humean orthodoxy. But let us leave that aside for the moment, and turn to the other form of anti-Humeanism. This is the view that belief alone is capable of motivating action. I argued for this view in the first three chapters of my *Moral Reasons* (1993). I accepted there (for most cases, at least[3]) the Humean view that motivation requires a combination of two distinct elements in the agent, but held that both could be beliefs. On my view, a desire is never a necessary part of what motivates. So we have two beliefs which together motivate. One of these is about how things are, and the other is about how they would be if the action were successfully performed. I called this view 'pure cognitivism'. (I argue for this position more formally in Chapter 4 below, but here lay out the bare bones of the thing.)

What has pure cognitivism to say about the role of desire in motivation? Does it deny altogether the need for desire? This would be unwise. For the core of the Humean distinction between belief and desire is captured in contemporary debate by the distinction between two directions of fit, as we have seen. The crucial point here is the availability of an a priori argument that for motivation one needs two distinct states, one with each direction of fit. Intentional action is only comprehensible if one can attribute to the agent some views about how things are and some views about how they are to be should the action be successful. Let us suppose that these 'views' are both beliefs. Still, the agent is motivated by those beliefs, and if so, he is in a state whose success conditions consist in things coming to be as, in that state, he conceives of them as to be. Such a state is a desire, not a belief, since the success conditions for a belief consist in things already being as they are there conceived. This is the present form of the original Humean claim that one needs both belief and desire. Pure cognitivism has a choice between denying the need for a state with each direction of fit and allowing the need for a desire as essential to motivation.

The move that I made, in response to this dilemma, was to allow that wherever there is motivation, there will be desire, but to deny

---

[3] The reason for this qualification is that it is possible for an action to be motivated by a single state of the agent—one belief rather than two; see Dancy (1993, ch. 2.6).

that the desire was a part of what motivates. The 'motivating state of the agent' itself consists entirely of beliefs, on my account; in fact such a state will normally consist of two beliefs. But where there is motivation, there is desire, since a desire is a state of being motivated. So I allowed the a priori argument that there is a need for two distinct states, one with each direction of fit, if there is to be motivation, but I removed desire entirely from the centre-stage position that it occupies in classical Humeanism. Desire never motivates, on my account. (If one is thirsty, one is motivated by the prospect of drinking.) But there can be no motivation without desire.

Psychologism and Anti-psychologism in the Theory of Motivating Reasons

Pure cognitivism accepts two central features of the Humean picture. The first of these is the asymmetry of belief and desire, i.e. the fact that belief and desire play quite different roles in motivation; this is captured in the distinction between two directions of fit. Pure cognitivism accepts that asymmetry, in accepting that what belief does desire cannot do, and vice versa. But it rejects the characteristic Humean stress on the dominance of desire in the generation of motivation. Desire is not the leading partner in anything, even though desire is a state that is out to change the world to be the way it wants, while belief is merely out to represent the world as it is.

Pure cognitivism also accepts the Humean claim that desire is an independent existence, with its own phenomenology. Desires occur, and they may have a distinctive 'feel', at least on occasion (the strong ones, probably). Their occurrence is required for motivation, but this is not surprising, since to desire is just to be motivated, and being motivated can have a distinctive feel.

There is, however, a further thing that pure cognitivism took unexamined from Humeanism, and this is much more significant than the two mentioned above. This is the idea that the theory of motivating states, as conceived by Humeans, constitutes or is the theory of acting for a reason—the theory of motivating reasons. To put it another way, Humeans presume that the theory of motivation is the theory of motivating reasons, and that this theory is to be written in terms of motivating states of the agent. The question

we were debating was whether such reasons could be beliefs—
whether a belief alone could be a reason for acting, in particular a
moral belief—or whether there needed also to be a desire. If desire
dominates belief in motivation, then it would be true to say that
our desires are the 'real' reasons why we act. If not, beliefs could
be reasons too, reasons as real as the desires. But this debate is pre-
missed on something itself hidden but still eminently debatable,
namely that our motivating reasons are psychological states of ourselves. I call this view psychologism. We were not arguing about
psychologism; we took it for granted, and argued only about which
psychological states were involved, and in which combinations.

As soon as one sees this, new possibilities swing into view. Are
any motivating reasons psychological states of the agent? Even the
most cursory glance at the sorts of reason we actually give, in
explaining either our own actions or those of others, reveals that
while some certainly seem to be characterized in terms of a psychological state of the agent, others equally certainly do not. We
say 'I am giving you this medicine because I believe that it will
reduce your temperature'; but we also say 'I stayed in because it
was raining', or 'We are going to sit outside because the sun has
come out'. Some reason-givings offer a belief of the agent as a
reason, then, in a way which might indeed be understood as a reference to a psychological state of the agent, but some offer something that seems not be a state of the agent at all, but a state of
affairs (the sun has come out); and there is a world of difference
between these. If the reason that motivates is the thing specified on
the right-hand side of the 'because' in 'I did it because p', many
such reasons are apparently not psychological states of the agent.
If reasons that motivate are all psychological states of the agent,
by contrast, no reasons are properly (i.e. fully) specifiable in the
form 'A acted because p'; the proper form will be 'A acted because
A believed that p', or something of that sort.

Internalism and Externalism in the Theory of Normative Reasons

Our understanding of this distinction is owed to Bernard Williams.
Internalism is a view about normative reasons, and it holds that an
agent A only has a good reason to ϕ if, were A to know all the relevant facts, and deliberate rationally, A would be motivated to ϕ.
The idea is that we start from A as he now is, with his existing set

of desires, or motivations, but supposedly not yet motivated to ϕ; and we ask whether, starting from there, A would become motivated to ϕ if he were to know all the relevant facts, and deliberate rationally. If the answer is no, A has no reason *as things stand* to ϕ.[4] Internalism, then, imposes a necessary condition on any supposed normative reason.

Calling this suggested necessary condition for having a reason 'motivation in condition C', we could more snappily express internalism as the view that A only has a reason to ϕ if A would be motivated to ϕ in condition C. Externalism about normative reasons is the claim that it is possible to have a good reason even when one would not be motivated accordingly in condition C.[5]

Internalism and externalism, so understood, are not views in the theory of motivation. They are views about the relation between good reasons and motivation. Internalism, understood as above, amounts to a motivational constraint on good reasons; something can only be a good reason for me if it is related to what I would want if I deliberated rationally and knew the relevant facts, starting from where I now am. Internalism therefore specifies a necessary condition on normative reasons. We cannot suppose that there are such reasons without specifying which agents they are reasons for, and no such attribution of a reason to an agent is true unless that agent would be suitably motivated in condition C. So we

---

[4] Even if A does at present have desires that the action would subserve. Note that Parfit (1997: 100) defines internalism disjunctively. According to him, it is the claim that 'for it to be true that (R) we have a reason to do something, it must be true that either (D) doing this thing might help to fulfil one of our present intrinsic desires, or (M) if we knew the relevant facts, and deliberated rationally, we would be motivated to do this thing'. Parfit's disjunctive version is untrue to the position that Williams originally presented. Williams wrote as follows, using 'S' to represent the agent's subjective motivational set, i.e. roughly the agent's desires: 'A member of S, D, will not give A a reason for ϕ-ing if either the existence of D is dependent on false belief, or A's belief in the relevance of ϕ-ing to the satisfaction of D is false' (1980: 103). On this account, a desire that does not satisfy the subjunctive condition (M) is incapable of, as we might put it, 'sustaining' a reason; on Parfit's account, satisfying condition (D) is enough for the sustaining of a reason. So Parfit's internalist would have to allow that if I do desire to drink what is in this glass, I have at least some reason to drink it, even though I would have no desire to drink it at all if I knew what it really contained. Williams's internalist need not allow this. This matter begins to make a difference early in Ch. 2.

[5] The formulations of internalism and externalism here concern the claim that an agent has a reason—some reason, one might say. For internalist accounts of the condition under which a specific feature F is a reason for A, or gives A a reason, see the beginning of Ch. 2.

cannot say, for instance, that there is a reason for anyone to be concerned about the needs of the homeless, unless we can show that
all agents whatever would be motivated accordingly in condition
C. Could all agents be got, starting from where they now are, to be
motivated by thoughts about the homeless, if they thought harder
and knew more? Somehow I doubt it.

Desire-Based and Value-Based Normative Reasons

This distinction is much harder to characterize, since there has been
no authoritative discussion of it. The desire-based view seems to be
that all normative reasons are 'provided' by desires of the agent,
while the value-based view is that some reasons, at least, are provided by ('grounded in') values such as the value of achievement,
of pleasure, of friendship, or whatever.[6] As such, these two views
seem to be about the metaphysical ground for a reason—about
what creates or generates it. They are not about necessary conditions for something to be a good reason for a particular agent—or
at least, they are not directly about that. The 'grounding' or 'pro-
viding' relation is different from, stronger than, and much more
interesting than the much weaker relation of 'being a necessary
condition for the existence of'. This point seems occasionally to
escape Derek Parfit's attention in his masterly typology of theoretical positions in this area, to which I am much indebted and
which essentially I am using here (Parfit 1997). He makes the following claims, all within three pages (pp. 128–30):

---

[6] There is the intermediate possibility that all reasons are desire-based, without
the desires concerned needing to belong to the agents who have the reasons. We
might think that every reason for action is eventually grounded in the desires
of someone or other, but that that person need not be the agent in the case. Con-
trariwise, as Lewis Carroll would say, the value-based view might go 'agent-centred'
and claim that all reasons for *A* are grounded in what is of value for or to *A*, rather
than in what is of value *tout court*. This shows that in considering the relation
between internalism and the distinction between desire-based and value-based
reasons we need to bear two questions in mind. The first is whether we are dealing
with a necessary condition for a reason or with the possible grounds for reasons.
The second is whether that which stands as condition, or as ground, is to be thought
of in an 'agent-centred' way or not. The desire-based view, as I have characterized
it in the text, concerns grounds, but in an agent-centred way; the value-based view,
as characterized, concerns grounds, but in an agent-neutral way. A neutral version
of the desire-based view would distance it noticeably from internalism, which is
clearly agent-centred. But it is normal to think of the desire-based view in an agent-
centred way, i.e. as grounding reasons for *A* in desires of *A*'s.

Internalist theories are desire-based.

According to many Internalists, all reasons are provided by desires.

On Internalist theories, the source of all reasons is something that is not itself normative: it is the fact that we have some desire.

When we have a reason to do something, this reason is not provided by, and does not require, the fact that after Internalist deliberation we would want to do this thing.

Parfit here seems to suggest both that all internalists believe in desire-based reasons, and that most do but some do not. He also suggests both that a desire-based reason is one based on the fact that we have some desire, and that it is one based on the desire itself. Most important, however, is the distinction that he draws in the last quoted sentence above, between a reason being 'provided by' some fact about the effect of internalist deliberation and its 'requiring' that fact. Talk of 'requiring' is talk of a necessary condition.

Internalism does not need to claim anything more than a necessary condition for something to be a reason if it is to serve Bernard Williams' original purpose, which was to show that if one cannot be taken from one's present motivational state, understood roughly as a set of present desires, to a state in which one has an appropriate desire, one has no good reason at all. Internalism can restrict itself to asserting that if our desires were different, we would have different reasons. It need not identify our desires, actual or hypothetical, with our reasons, nor suppose that our reasons are given by, or provided by, our desires; nor need it claim, as Parfit at one point puts it, that our desires are the 'source of' our reasons.[7] Internalism of this limited and non-reductive sort[8] amounts to a constraint on the reasons that we have, and to no more than that.[9] Now

[7] The same goes for facts about our desires, rather than those desires themselves.
[8] I do not mean by this to suggest that this sort of limited internalism is the only non-reductive form of internalism. One can claim that for A to be motivated in condition C is both necessary and sufficient for A to have a reason, while still stressing that the fact that A has such reason is a distinctive further fact, over and above the facts about actual and potential desires or motivations of A's. The same applies if one takes internalism as a theory about what gives us our reasons (the grounds for reasons) rather than merely about conditions under which we have reasons.
[9] Reductive forms of internalism are of course different in this respect, but only because, being reductive, they suppose a far tighter relation between (R)

if we take internalism in this way, Parfit's claim that 'Internalist theories are desire-based theories' becomes a mistake. We can abandon desire-based theories and still stick to this form of internalism.

Parfit writes:

According to normative Internalism:

> (A) Some acts really are rational. There are facts about these acts, and their relations to our motivation, which give us reasons to act in these ways. (p. 129)

But our limited internalism does not say this. What it says is rather:

> (A*) Some acts really are rational. There are facts about these acts, and their relation to our motivation, without which we would not have reasons to act in those ways.

The characterization of internalism in terms of 'giving reasons' introduces a claim that goes beyond A*. There is, then, a possible version of internalism that is weaker than the one that Parfit is expressing here, that allows that reasons are never psychological states of the agent, or 'facts about his motivation', but that still insists on a certain relation to desires of the agent if anything is to be a reason for that agent. It requires that any reason mesh in a certain way with the motivation of the agent for whom it is a reason, without demanding that such motivation create, generate, or be the source of the reason. We do not argue against this view by showing that some reasons are not 'desire-based'. The only objection to it that I can find in Parfit's paper—and, like many of Parfit's best objections, it is perfectly simple—is that according to internalism, 'those who were sufficiently ruthless, or amoral, would have no duties, and . . . could not be held to be acting wrongly' (pp. 102–3). To run this objection we have to hold that if someone is acting wrongly, he has at least some reason not to do what he is doing, whatever his actual or potential desires.

---

and either (D) or (M); this tighter relation derives from the reductiveness of the internalism, not from the internalism itself. (For (R), (D), and (M), see n. 4 above.) This will be true whether reductive internalism comes in the analytic or the non-analytic form, i.e. whether it claims that the meaning of (R) is given by the disjunction of (D) and (M), or merely that the fact reported by (R) is the same fact as that reported by the disjunction of (D) or (M). For all these distinctions, see Parfit (1997).

6. *Looking Back and Looking Forward*

This chapter has been largely concerned with laying the ground for what follows, and constructing the terms in which the debate is to take place. I have to apologize for trying my readers' patience with the plethora of distinctions that it has contained. The excuse, of course, is that what is to come cannot be understood without at least some grasp on those distinctions, and I have, of course, to make it as clear as possible how I understand them. To lay my cards on the table, then, the next two chapters concern the possible grounds for a good practical reason. I will be arguing that such reasons are not based on the agent's desires (Chapter 2), and that they are not based on the agent's beliefs either (Chapter 3). In Chapter 4 I turn away from good reasons to the topic of motivation, and argue that pure cognitivism is the soundest form of psychologism in the theory of motivation as standardly conceived. In Chapter 5, however, I argue that we should not accept any form of psychologism anyway. We should attempt to understand the reasons that motivate us as features of the situation rather than as features of ourselves. Chapters 6–7 continue in this vein, building up the position I prefer and replying to objections, and the final chapter discusses whether the account of motivating reasons that I have given is either itself causal or at least compatible with a causal account.

APPENDIX

The History of the Distinction between Motivating and Normative Reasons

One of the main thrusts of this book will be that those who have recently worked on the distinction between good reasons and those that motivate have managed to mangle it more or less out of all recognition. They have turned a distinction between two contexts in which we use the notion of a reason into a distinction between two *sorts* of reason, in such a way as to tear apart something that needs to be kept in one piece if intentional action is not to be rendered unintelligible. In supposing that there are two sorts of reason, motivating ones and normative ones, they often claim historical precedent. In this Appendix I argue that those alleged precedents are not worth appealing to. The earliest propounder of the distinction, supposedly, was Francis Hutcheson, who wrote:

When we ask the reason of an action, we sometimes mean 'What truth shews a quality in the action, exciting the agent to do it?' Thus, why does a luxurious man pursue wealth? The reason is given by this truth, 'Wealth is useful to purchase pleasures'. Sometimes for a reason of actions we shew the truth expressing a quality, engaging our approbation. Thus the reason of hazarding life in just war is that 'it tends to preserve our honest countrymen, or evidences public spirit'. The former sort of reasons we will call exciting, and the latter justifying. Now we shall find that all exciting reasons presuppose instincts and affections, and the justifying presuppose a moral sense. (1728: 404)

The first thing to say is that if this is really a version of the distinction between normative and motivating reasons, there seems to be no justification for thinking of all 'exciting reasons' as given by truths. For an agent may be 'excited', i.e. motivated, by a false conception of the situation and the prospects it offers. A man may pursue wealth on the grounds that wealth increases security, little reckoning that the wealthy man is the one who is the target of predators, so that wealth actually diminishes rather than increases security. (I am assuming for the purposes of the example that this is in fact the case.) If the exciting reason is that wealth increases security, Hutcheson is wrong if he supposes that all reasons are given by truths. This matter will become significant later on. I will only say here that Hutcheson appears not to be in favour of a rewriting of the supposed exciting reason which would make it the truth that the agent believed that wealth increases security rather than the falsehood that wealth increases security.

It may be, however, that Hutcheson intends both exciting and justifying reasons to come in the category of normative reasons, which do all need to be true—or at least to be 'shewn' by truths. If it is true that wealth is useful to purchase pleasures, this may be thought to be a good reason for pursuing wealth, at least for those whose inclinations lie in the direction of the luxurious. Understood in this way, the exciting reasons are just those good reasons for acting that appeal to 'instincts and affections' such as a predilection for luxury rather than to our moral sense. Prudential reasons will be exciting reasons, on this account, rather than justifying ones. Hutcheson is not drawing the distinction between normative and motivating reasons at all. He is distinguishing between two sorts of normative reason.

Hutcheson's distinction was revived in recent times by William Frankena:

It seems to me, at any rate, that we must distinguish two kinds of reasons for action, 'exciting reasons' and 'justifying reasons', to use Hutcheson's terms. When *A* asks 'Why should I give Smith a ride?', *B* may give answers of two different kinds. He may say, 'Because you promised to', or he may say, 'Because, if you do, he will remember you in his will'. In the first case, he offers a justification of the action, in the second a motive for doing it. In other words, *A*'s 'Why should I . . . ?' and 'Why ought I . . . ?' are ambiguous questions . . . 'Should' and 'ought' likewise have two meanings (at least) which are prima facie distinct: a moral one and a motivational one.

Thus a motive is one kind of reason for action, but not all reasons for action are motives. Perhaps we should distinguish between reasons for acting and reasons for regarding an action as right or justified. It is plausible to identify reasons for acting with motives, i.e. with considerations which will or may move one to action . . . but it is not plausible to identify motives with reasons for regarding an action as morally right or obligatory. (1958: 44)

Like Hutcheson, Frankena offers here two kinds of good reason for action, i.e. two kinds of normative reason. The first is a moral reason, and the second a prudential one. He is not distinguishing between the reasons for which we act and the reasons in favour of acting. He is distinguishing between two sorts of reason in favour of acting. But Frankena adds to what Hutcheson had to say something quite distinct and idiosyncratic. One sort of reason he calls a motive, and he supposes that when we speak of this kind of reason, the word 'reason' has a 'motivational' meaning. Moral reasons for acting are to be understood in a quite different way, however, as reasons for regarding an action as morally right. They are not motives, and the word 'reason' in the moral context does not have a 'motivational' meaning. It concerns reasons for regarding, i.e. for believing something or other, I suppose, rather than for acting. Moral reasons, it turns out, are not really reasons for action at all.

Now this announcement of Frankena's has appeared from nowhere. What justification could there be for insisting that moral reasons are not 'motivational', and that moral reasons are reasons for regarding an action as right *rather than* reasons for doing it? Frankena just announces that an ethical justification for an action is not what he calls a motive for doing it, as if to give a good moral reason for doing it is not to give one a motive to do it. This can only rest on some antecedent conception of what a motive is.

What is more, one can argue that there is a general distinction to be drawn between the reasons why it is the case that *p* and any reasons there may be for believing that *p*. Suppose, for instance, that a respected and wise person (if such can still be found) has come to the conclusion that a certain course of action is morally dubious. This is perhaps some reason to believe that that course of action *is* dubious. But it is not itself among the reasons why that course is dubious. Those features that are the reasons why the course is dubious, such as, perhaps, that it involves an element of deceit, may also play the role of reasons for believing it to be dubious; but that role is a secondary role, which can be played by other considerations that are not themselves moral reasons. (This point is a general point, not especially a point about moral reasons. That the hedgehogs are hibernating early may be a reason to believe we will have a dry winter, but it is probably not among the reasons why the winter will be dry; the latter will more probably be facts about climatic shift, or whatever.) We should not, then, be tempted by any general analysis of moral reasons as reasons for judgement rather than for action.

Of course we should remember that Frankena's discussion of Hutcheson's distinction is produced in the course of an argument about the rights and wrongs of what is called an 'internalistic' conception of moral judgement, the conception according to which it is impossible for an agent to make a sincere moral judgement and not to be motivated accordingly. (This is Moral Belief Internalism, in Parfit's typology, to be kept severely distinct from the Williams-type internalism I have been discussing above; see again Parfit 1997.) Frankena's argument against this internalism is certainly helped by imposing on the debate the idea that moral reasons are only reasons for regarding an action as right, leaving the question whether to do that action as yet unaddressed. But this imposition is surely contentious in general, and especially so in that context.

It is one thing to announce that moral reasons are not motives, and another to announce that other reasons, such as prudential ones, are motives. The purpose of claiming that other reasons are motives consists, I think, in the underlying idea that being a motive consists in a tripartite relation between the consideration that is the motive, the agent, and the action, while being a moral reason consists only in a bipartite relation between the consideration that is the reason and the action, the relation of making it true that the action is right or justified or wrong or unjustified. A motive involves the agent in a way that a 'mere' reason does not. We might suppose that there cannot be motives that nobody has got, since a motive is essentially something belonging to an agent; but there can be moral reasons that nobody has got, since the status of such a reason as a reason does not depend on any relation to an individual agent. Reasons can exist in a sort of void, but motives cannot. I do not recommend this picture at all, but something like it may underlie Frankena's pronouncements.

I leave this matter here, only noting that to call non-moral reasons motives is to open a door, the door that leads to thinking of desires as motives, or of motives as desires, and hence to thinking of ordinary practical reasons as essentially related to desire. This matter is the topic of the next chapter.

I have argued in this Appendix that the simple distinction between reasons that motivate and normative or good reasons which I am interested in is not to be found in either Hutcheson or Frankena. In fact, the best account of the distinction that I know of is to be found in Baier (1958: 148–62).[10] Baier's general picture of the relation between the motivating and the normative (for which he uses the term 'justifying') is very congenial to the views I shall go on to propound. In particular, he is careful not to talk of two *types* of reason, but of two contexts in which the word 'reason' is used. These are the context of explanation and the context of deliberation and justification. Baier suggests that in both contexts we specify facts (or, in the context of explanation, maybe just supposed facts; see p. 159) that are taken to be good reasons for acting. In the case of the context of explanation, it will be the agent who supposes this; in the context of justification, the enterprise of justification requires that the facts offered be good reasons. Baier is especially interested in using this distinction to explain what he takes to be the mistaken view that facts can be intrinsically motivating. He explains this by imputing to those who hold it a sort of conflation of the two uses of 'reason'. To be mentioned as a reason in the context of motivation, a (supposed) fact must indeed motivate. (Things are even worse if one speaks of reasons as motives. Baier writes (p. 157), 'If reasons are not distinguished from motives, it is obvious that . . . if they are facts, then the moving power must somehow be lodged in these facts.') But to be a good reason, i.e. to be mentioned as a reason in the context of justification, the fact that is the reason need not be motivating anybody at all. Normative reasons, therefore, are not intrinsically motivating.

The fact that the supposed history of the distinction between good reasons and those that motivate turns out not to be quite as generally supposed should not disconcert us. As I see it, the basis of the distinction, when it is properly understood, is not itself either philosophically deep or significant, nor does it need any great acumen to discover or understand, in the ordinary sense of 'understand'. It is what philosophers have said about the distinction, that is, the castles that they have erected on it, that are philosophically challenging, for very significant matters depend on our philosophical accounts of motivation, of good reasons, and of the relation between them. The construction of a distorted history is just one sign that things are going wrong.

Hutcheson's distinction amounted to a general distinction between moral and other good reasons, related to a (contentious) distinction between instincts and affections, on the one hand, and a 'moral sense', on the other. Frankena's distinction again started from a general distinction between moral and other good reasons, one which was itself quite inca-

[10] I should also cite Joseph Raz's distinction between guiding and explanatory reasons, discussed in his introduction to Raz (1978).

pable of sustaining the position he then erected upon it. The rights and wrongs of the views of these two writers will not occupy us further. The distinction between moral and other reasons is not the topic of this book, whose general assumption is that there may not be a huge difference between the two.

Reasons and Desires

1. *Internalism and Desire-Based Reasons*

How best should we understand the relation between internalism and the thesis that all the good reasons we have are based on or grounded in our own desires (the DBR thesis, from now on)? These positions seem both to be part of one and the same larger story, because of their common focus on desires of the agent. How then should we try to combine them?

I suggested in Chapter 1 that we should take internalism as a specification of a necessary condition for anything to count as a good reason, not as a claim about the grounds for reasons. Any reason we have must be appropriately related to desires (or perhaps, more generally, motivations) that we would acquire, or retain, under condition *C*. Williams is right, it seems to me, to claim that the actual desires or motivations of the agent are not in themselves relevant here. A feature may be appropriately related to an actual desire, but it is not thereby fitted to stand as a good reason for the agent unless that desire would survive the process of re-education and sound reasoning. This is because, as Williams notes, we do have to retain and in some way substantiate the normative status of reasons. Our actual desires cannot serve to ground this normative status unless they would themselves survive the sort of normative test that is involved in what I have called condition *C*, i.e. in asking whether they would survive an increase in knowledge, a decrease in error, and improved deliberation. Williams writes:

An important part of the internalist account lies in the idea of there being a 'sound deliberative route' from the agent's existing *S* to his ϕ-ing. It is important that even on the internalist view a statement of the form '*A* has reason to ϕ' has *normative force*. Unless a claim to the effect that an agent has a reason to ϕ can go beyond what that agent is already motivated to do—that is, go beyond his already being motivated to ϕ—then certainly the terms will have too narrow a definition. '*A* has a reason to ϕ' means more than '*A* is presently disposed to ϕ'. (1995: 36)

And, we might add, it also means less than this, since it can be true when the latter is false. I conclude that Williams's internalist should think of desires we actually have as irrelevant unless we would retain them under condition C.[1]

In my earlier discussion, I considered only how an internalist should deal with the claim that the agent *A* has some reason or other. But we need also an internalist specification of the condition required for a specific feature to be a reason. Suppose that the fact that the train is about to leave is a reason for him to run. If this is so, internalism tells us, it must be that if better informed and reasoning well, he would have a desire that would be subserved by running. Here, then, is a tentative and rather awkward characterization of internalism in its most general form:

> That it is the case that *p* is a good reason for *A* to ϕ *only if* there is some *e* such that in condition C *A* would desire *e* and, given that *p*, ϕ-ing subserves the prospect of *e*'s being realized (or continuing to be realized).

In the example before us, *e* is the end of catching the train, ϕ-ing is running, and *p* is 'the train is about to leave'. In this way we understand the idea that the fact that the train is about to leave is a reason for *A* to run. Note that the internalist has no need to *identify* our reasons with the desires that we would have in condition C. Those reasons can still be perfectly ordinary considerations such as that the train is about to leave, which are enabled to be the reasons they are by the relation in which they stand to desires that we would have if we thought harder and knew more.

---

[1] There is a complication here. There are two conceptions of a sound deliberative route. The first is the 'substantive' conception, which amounts to whatever route is a sound one, understood *de dicto*. This conception of a sound route is clearly normative; it wears its normativity on its face. There is a distinct conception, however, which we might call 'procedural', and which simply lists the inference patterns that are taken to be sound, one by one. Insisting that a desire should survive all inferences drawn according to those patterns is not so obviously normative. So Williams's attempt to retain the normativity of reasons by appeal to the notion of a sound deliberative route is better served if he can appeal to the substantive conception rather than just the procedural one. (Parfit makes a different use of the terms 'substantive' and 'procedural' in Parfit 1997: 100–1.)

When we think about the grounding relation that turns something into a reason for a particular agent, however, defenders of the
DBR thesis may well feel that only *actual* desires can stand in that
relation to a reason. After all, to anticipate a little, the overall
picture we are being offered here is something like this. Nothing is
in its own right an end; there are no 'ends in themselves'. Prospects
become ends for us when we adopt them as *our* ends, which we do,
effectively, by desiring them. Reasons stem from this creation of
ends by desire; once we have adopted an end, we have reason to
do what will subserve that end, reason that we did not have before.
Now it seems that on this picture ends cannot be created by desires
that we do not yet have, but would only have in condition *C*. A
desire needs actually to exist if it is to be capable of turning what
is not an end in itself into an end for us. So the DBR thesis should
read like this:

> If its being the case that *p* is a good reason for *A* to *φ*, *this is
> because* there is some *e* such that *A* actually desires *e* and,
> given that *p*, *φ*-ing subserves the prospect of *e*'s being realized
> (or continuing to be realized).

So the best way to combine internalism with the DBR thesis seems
to be to say that our reasons are grounded in our *actual* desires, but
only if those desires would survive under condition *C*. Desires we
do not have but would have under condition *C* cannot ground
actual reasons for us, however; we have to get the desires before
we can have the reasons.

This combination has several strengths. First, it can allow that we
have reasons that we are not aware of. We have such reasons when,
not being aware of some relevant fact, we fail to recognize that *φ*-
ing would subserve a desire we have and which we would still have
in condition *C*. Second, it can allow that we can be wrong in taking
ourselves to have a reason; this happens when we have a desire that
we fail to recognize would not survive under condition *C*, or when
we falsely believe that doing this would subserve a desire of ours
that would survive under condition *C*. Third, the combined position is still worth calling a form of internalism. For the question
whether *I* have a reason to do this action is still beholden to facts
about my current motivational state, which Williams calls 'my
present *S*'. I only have a reason if I can be got by a 'sound deliberative route' from my present *S* to an *S* in which I am motivated

appropriately. This constraint should serve perfectly well Williams' general purpose of undermining what he calls 'bluff' about reasons (1981: 111). No matter how strongly someone may press a supposed reason on you, you can always resist them by showing that at present you have no desire that would be subserved by doing what they want you to do, and you could not be got to have such a desire by any 'sound deliberative route'.

Here then we have a complex position with a significant internal rationale and a common focus on the notion of a desire. What alternative position might we take? The suggestion most common in the literature, and which I will support here, is that instead of being based on or grounded in desires, our normative reasons are based on values.

Though I shall be taking this line, it is worth pointing out that it is not the only possible one. It is a substantial position in normative theory to suppose that all reasons are founded on values, even once one has rejected the opposing claim that they are all founded on desires. Within the normative realm, considered as a whole, there are two potentially distinct parts. There is the evaluative, and there is the deontic. The evaluative is the realm of value, of good and bad, of evil and benign. The deontic is the realm of 'oughts'— of requirements, of demands, of right and wrong, and of reasons. (A reason is a consideration that one ought not to ignore, even if things would go better if one did ignore it.) Those who suppose that reasons must rest on values if they do not rest on desires are implicitly imposing a certain layer-cake structure on the normative. At the bottom there are the features that generate value; above that there is the value so generated, and above that are the reasons and requirements that are laid on us by the prospect of value, and only by that. My point here is just that this is a very contentious picture, and that I do not want to bind myself to it by anything that follows. In one form or another, it is the picture offered us by G. E. Moore. In his *Principia Ethica* (1903) he defined the right as that which is most productive of the good; in his later *Ethics* (1912) he seems to have taken the weaker view that the only way an action can get to be right is by being productive of the most good. Either way, these suggestions have a distinctively consequentialist air, and deontologists are likely to find them disputable. The obvious alternative possibility is that some reasons are directly grounded on the facts, i.e. on the lower-level features that also function as the ground for value, rather than indirectly via an intermediate level of value.

Others are less cautious. Parfit, for instance, writes:

If we consider only reasons for acting, Internalism may seem to be broadly right, or to contain most of the truth. But the most important reasons are not merely, or mainly, reasons for acting. They are also reasons for having the desires on which we act. These are reasons to want some thing, for its own sake, which are provided by facts about this thing. Such reasons we can call value-based.[2] (1997: 127–8)

E. J. Bond writes:

There is a connection between reasons and value that seems plain at the start, for to believe that one has a reason for or against doing something, in the context of deliberation, is to believe that there is something of value or worth to be achieved (or preserved) by doing it or not doing it, as the case may be. (1983: 2)

Warren Quinn discusses a view he calls objectivism, by contrast to the 'subjectivist' view that evaluative judgements give us reasons only because of their non-cognitive force, which he thinks of as a sort of non-cognitive content. He writes:

Objectivists . . . see things very differently. They agree that moral thought, at least when it is correct, provides reasons for action. But they think that it does so only because of its cognitive content. What rationalizes or makes sense of the pursuit of a goal, they assert, is some way in which the goal in question seems good. And what rationalizes or makes sense of strict conformity to a principle is some way in which it seems that one can act well only by following it. (1993*a*: 232)

We should not allow ourselves to move *immediately* from the sound thought that some of our reasons are the reasons they are because of their content rather than because of any desires of ours, to the more contentious claim that such reasons are value-based. More

---

[2] Since he wrote Parfit (1997), Parfit has moved towards the appealing view that for something to be valuable is for it to have a feature that gives us a reason to want or to choose it (or promote it or preserve it or do it or . . .). Thomas Scanlon, who propounds this view in Scanlon (1999), calls it the 'buck-passing view', since it sees value as passing the buck to the features that give us our reasons. I raise some doubts about the buck-passing view in Dancy (2000*b*). But if it were true, Parfit's suggestion that all reasons stem from values becomes less contentious, once re-expressed as the view that all reasons are grounded in the existence of reason-giving features. The values would simply pass the buck to the features grounding the reasons, and there would be no distinction between a value-based reason and a content-based reason.

generally, we should demand further persuasion before we allow that the deontic is grounded in the evaluative, or that non-desire-based reasons are grounded in value. Which is not to say that such persuasion may not eventually be forthcoming.

2. *Against Desire-Based Reasons*

I know of four ways of arguing against the DBR thesis:

- (*a*) by counter-example;
- (*b*) by showing that the DBR thesis is internally inconsistent;
- (*c*) by establishing that desire is based on reasons, not reasons on desires;
- (*d*) by appeal to some view in the theory of motivating reasons (triangulation).

The first method can be effective, though it is vulnerable to the response which consists in stubbornly insisting that there must be a desire in there somewhere, even if on first appearances there is not. We might try to say, for instance, that there are things that I do not want and could not be got to want, but which it would be better (for me?) if I did want. Parfit says that as well as reasons for action '[there] are also reasons to want some thing, for its own sake, which are provided by facts about this thing' (1997: 128). But I pass over this sort of approach as inconclusive even if the stubborn response to it fails. The reason why it is inconclusive is that, even though it might persuade us, it cannot provide what we really need. For it is not as if the debate about the DBR thesis is just about how many of our reasons are based on desires. It is not as if some people have started looking at our reasons, and noticed, almost by counting them, that most of them are desire-based, and then gone on to infer that they all are. Nor is it, on the other side, that though one recognizes that plenty of reasons are desire-based, one thinks there are probably a few that are not—a few stubborn counter-examples to what would otherwise be an exceptionless generalization about the grounds of our practical reasons. The real issue between attackers and defenders of the DBR thesis concerns how to conceive the relation between reasons and desires. Defenders of the thesis think that the thesis is true of all reasons, not because it is true of most and so probably true of all, but because of what they think must be the correct account of the relation between reasons and desires. Those who attack the thesis do so because they dispute that account. They may be encouraged, in doing so, by noticing stubborn counter-examples to it. But more than counter-examples is needed if the *philosophical* picture on which the DBR thesis rests is to be undermined.

What this means is that it is not just a matter of counting heads. Since the real debate is about the proper conception of the relation between reasons and desires, it is going to be possible to argue (which it would not if we were simply counting heads) that some reasons are not desire-based, and that this somehow shows that none are.

The second method is more attractive, and since it has the charms of simplicity, we can call it the Simple Argument. It has one premiss, and a conclusion:

> *Premiss*: A desire to ϕ cannot itself give us any reason to ϕ. For if ϕ-ing is silly or even just not very sensible, wanting to ϕ does not make it less silly or a bit more sensible.

> *Conclusion*: If a desire to ϕ gives us no reason to ϕ, it can give us no reason to do other actions either; in particular, it can give us no reason to do those actions that subserve ϕ-ing (either as means to ϕ-ing as end, or in some other way).

The Premiss of the Simple Argument is easy to establish. This is partly because it is so obviously true. But, more importantly, it is agreed on all hands. This may not be so immediately obvious. But remember the broader picture that sustains the DBR thesis. No prospect is an end in itself, we are told. A prospect is converted into an end for me by my adopting it as such, which I do by coming to desire it. This does not mean that we now have a reason to pursue that end when we did not have one before. We cannot give ourselves a reason to pursue that end by adopting it as an end. But we do now have some reasons that we had not before, namely reasons to do the things that will promote or subserve that end, either as means to it, or in some other way. On this story, which is the basic picture underlying the DBR thesis, the Premiss of the Simple Argument is granted already.

The Conclusion of the Simple Argument, by contrast, is very much harder to show. Warren Quinn fails notably to show it. He writes that 'If my basic love of listening to music doesn't give me a reason to listen, then it doesn't, I think, give me a reason to take the record down [from the shelf]' (1993*a*: 237). This is indeed the position to be established. But Quinn says nothing further in its defence.[3] John Broome does not do much better. He writes:

Wanting X does not give you a reason to want A when A is actually X itself under another description. A fortiori, it does not give you a reason to want A when A is a mere means to X. If wanting X cannot give you a reason to want an act that is X itself, it cannot give you a reason to want an act that is more remote from X. (1997: 136)

What is wrong with these and other attempts to make the point by mere assertion is just that they beg the question against the theory of desire-based reasons. In standard formulations of this theory, as we have seen, no criticism is made of intrinsic desires, since these lie outside the realm of reasons. The theory itself claims that there are no reasons for or against intrinsic desires; one just has them or one doesn't. But which desires one does have, it says, can make a difference to how it is sensible for one to act. One's desire to ϕ can give one a reason to prefer one action to another if the first gives one more chance of ϕ-ing than does the second.

If this is the theory, what is wrong with it? What we want is to be given some reason to believe that the Simple Argument is sound. Quinn offered us no such reason, and Broome's use of the phrase 'a fortiori' seems to me to be just another attempt to assert that the second stage of the Simple Argument follows directly from the first stage. Broome's argument quoted above reads, paraphrased:

Wanting X does not give you a reason to want A when A is actually X itself under another description. A fortiori, it does

[3] This may appear to be a gross exaggeration, since there then follows a long argument to the effect that a mere urge to do X (or a desire conceived as a functional state) cannot rationalize doing X. What will rationalize an action will be the sort of evaluation that standardly accompanies such a state. But even if we allowed this, it does nothing to show that a person with a certain urge has no reason to take means to the satisfaction of that urge as an end. All that it shows is that having such an urge gives us no reason to do what we feel the urge to do. It remains open whether having the urge gives us a reason to do other things. If one wants to say that it is evaluation that rationalizes, it is easy to find an evaluation that will do the trick for the urge-based reasons theorist. For the action can be seen as having the valuable feature of being the thing whose occurrence would satisfy one's urge. This value will be conditional on the presence of the urge, but need not be identified with the value of urge satisfaction. (See Rabinowicz and Osterberg 1996.)

not give you a reason to want A when A is not X itself under another description.

Again, this seems to be not so much an argument as a statement of the position to be established. We need to look further.

We could understand the picture underlying the DBR thesis as consisting of two parts. The first part holds that desires convert what is not an end in itself into something that is an end for the agent—the desirer. The second part holds that a desire to ϕ gives us no reason to ϕ, but does give us a reason to do whatever will subserve ϕ-ing. What Broome tried to do was to use one of these against the other. His basic thought, I suppose, was that we can think of ϕ-ing as a limiting case of doing something that subserves ϕ-ing. For after all, if your goal is ϕ-ing, one of the best ways around of achieving this goal, if available, is just to ϕ. In such a case, ϕ-ing can be seen as a means to itself—as subserving itself. If so, then if the first part of the picture referred to above is true, the second part must be false.

There is, I think, a principled way in which the DBR thesis, and the picture that supports it, can be defended against any such attack. This involves appeal to what I call 'the advice point'. Suppose that some people come to you asking for advice about how to pursue a project that they have adopted. They have decided, say, to insulate their house so effectively that no sound whatever penetrates from outside. You might think that there is no reason whatever to adopt this project, and that the fact that they have adopted it does not mean that they now have a reason to pursue it that they did not have before. No reason to adopt it, therefore, and no reason to pursue it either. But if they are going to pursue this project, you might say, or now that they have adopted it and made it their project, they have a reason to take this means to it rather than that, since this one is markedly more likely to have the desired effect. If fibreglass insulation is both more effective, cheaper, and less damaging to people and the environment than is polystyrene, they have much more reason to use fibreglass than polystyrene. But the reason exists because this action best subserves a project that there is, we have admitted, no reason to pursue.

This little story is a sort of model of the Humean picture that underlies the DBR thesis. There is no reason to adopt this project, we say, but once one has adopted it, this gives one reasons that one did not have before. It seems to me that as a model this does appear perfectly coherent, and that until something has been said to unsettle that appearance, manœuvres like Broome's cannot be expected to be effective. We will have to find some way of dealing with the advice point if we want to wield any form of the Simple Argument.

With all these things in mind, I now offer an argument that is like Broome's in some ways, but which has far more detail in it. The hope is that thereby we can avoid simply begging the question against the DBR thesis. The argument is much influenced by the work of Raz, Scanlon, and Quinn.[4] Its overall aim is to show that no desire is a reason, and to argue from this that no reasons are desire-based.

The argument starts by noting the number and variety of desires that are immediately grounded, not in deeper, more basic desires, but in reasons. Most of the things we want, we want for a reason. This reason will usually be some good that we see in the thing that we want or in some other suitably related object. I want to learn how to do a proper vibrato on my double-bass because in this way I will be able to control it better, and so play baroque music as it ought to be played, not as if it was written in the late nineteenth century. I want to write this book because I think that the notion of a good reason is not well understood. These are comparatively grand aims, but there are also smaller ones. I want to buy some fresh fruit because I have some friends coming to supper and this will round the meal off nicely after the cheese. All these desires, and all desires of this sort, are grounded in reasons, real or apparent. Of course some people want something because they wrongly take it to promise some good, or because they wrongly suppose that there is a reason to want it, being right about what it promises but wrong that it is a good. In the relevant sense, however, their desires are still reason-based.[5]

---

[4] Raz (1986, 1998); Scanlon (1999); Quinn (1993*a*). See also Watson (1975).

[5] This claim may be confusing, since it is natural for those with Humean sympathies to say that these reasons are obviously desire-based, or at least can clearly be understood as such. But this is irrelevant at the present stage of the argument. The point is only that many desires are based on the recognition of some good. Humeans can insist either that the agent desires that good, or that to recognize a good is (in some way) to desire it. The former claim will turn out to be irrelevant, given the structure of the argument to come. The phenomenon of listlessness (accidie) gives us sufficient reason to reject the latter claim. I will argue in Ch. 4 that to desire is to be motivated. Given this, the fact that it is possible, notably but not only in states of severe depression, to think of something as a good but just not to care about it, not to be motivated by it at all, seems to establish that to recognize a good is not to desire it.

Are there any desires that are not reason-based? Two sorts of case are commonly cited: urges, and inclinations. Take the inclinations first. Often I do something just because I am that way inclined. Perhaps I wear this shirt today because I feel like it. Is this a case of a desire that is not based on a reason? No. There are perfectly good reasons for putting on this shirt. But they are not decisive, in the sense that there are equally good reasons for putting on a different one. Where the reasons are not decisive, I let inclination decide. But what I do, I have perfectly good reasons for doing, and I do it for those reasons. Inclinations are just desires that we have for inconclusive reasons.

Urges are rather different. To be effective as counter-examples to the general claim that desires are had for reasons, urges must be desires that we have, and do not have because there is some reason to be moved in this way (even if there is in fact such a reason) or because we see some good in that which we experience the urge to do. The commonly cited urges are not very effective examples of that sort of thing. For instance, the urge to eat another slice of cake, or to touch a woman's elbow, are surely grounded (in some way) in the idea that it would be good in some form to do these things. The only urges that would be effective as counter-examples are those which the person concerned entirely disavows, seeing no good in them whatever. But these are surely pathological (and hardly likely to stand at the bottom of all motivation). What is more to the point, they surely do not count as reasons for doing that which we experience the urge to do, since in announcing that we see nothing good in so acting, we have made it hard to say that we see or have some reason to act that way all the same. An urge of this sort is something that one has no reason to satisfy, though it may be the case that one will (be driven to) satisfy it.

The argument's second main claim is that if a desire is reason-based in this sort of way, the desire does not itself add to those reasons. If one desires something for a reason, it is not as if one then has more reason to do it than one had before. The desire, as Joseph Raz has written, is an endorsement of a reason that is independent of it (1986: 141), and that endorsement does not itself affect the stock of reasons.

Similarly, if someone wants something that there is no reason to want, his desire does not give him some reason for doing it, a reason that was not there before. If an action is silly, wanting to do it does not make it any the less silly. It may be that if one wants to do it, one is more likely to do it. But that is a different matter. (The same point as above *re* urges.)

So far I have spoken of a desire as a potential reason to do the thing desired, and decided that no desire can give us further reason to add to those (real or apparent) reasons that are already there, and to which the desire is a response. But could it be that though desires are not reasons to do the thing desired, they are reasons to do what will subserve the thing desired? Well, if we have no reason to ϕ, the fact that ψ-ing will make it easier to ϕ is no reason to ψ. This I think of as uncontroversial. Suppose now that though we have no reason to ϕ, we still want to do it. What difference could this make? Does it mean that the fact that ψ-ing will make it easier to ϕ now constitutes a reason to ψ, though we have no more reason to ϕ than before? Surely we are still facing the awkward point that the fact that ψ-ing will make it easier to ϕ is only a reason to ψ if we have some reason to ϕ.

The oddity involved in the claim that a desire to ϕ gives us a reason to do whatever subserves ϕ-ing, but no reason to ϕ itself, can be most clearly brought out by considering a case where I have every reason to avoid ϕ-ing, even though I have a yen to ϕ none the less. I hesitate to give an example of this, but the sort of one that springs to mind is some shameful act that would immediately bring my career and marriage to an end, but which I still have some desire to do. All agree that I have no reason to do this act, and every reason not to do it. In such a case, it seems perverse to claim that my desire to ϕ does add to the stock of reasons for ψ-ing just because ψ-ing subserves ϕ-ing, and so gives me good reason to do something because it subserves doing something that there is every reason not to do. I suggest that this makes no sense, so that if the desire to ϕ does not add to the reasons for ϕ-ing, it cannot add to the reasons for ψ-ing. Generalizing from this case to the more ordinary case where I have no reason to ϕ, but merely want to do so, I conclude that if desires do not add reasons in the primary way, they cannot add them in the secondary way either. Nor is the instrumental relation capable of generating extra normativity in its own right.

38 Reasons and Desires

Here is the structure of the argument just provided:

(1) Some desires are based on reasons; such desires stand on, rather than beneath, those reasons.
(2) A desire that is not based on reasons will be either an inclination or an urge.
(3) Inclinations are based on reasons (inconclusive ones).
(4) Some urges are based on reasons.
(5) An urge that is not based on a reason cannot stand as a reason for doing that which we have the urge to do.
(6) A desire that is based on reasons does not add to the reasons on which it is based.
(7) Where we have every reason not to ϕ, the fact that ψ-ing will subserve ϕ-ing cannot give us a reason to ψ.
(8) Where we have no reason to ϕ, the fact that ψ-ing will subserve ϕ-ing can be no reason to ψ, even where we desire to ϕ.

This, though brief, is an attempt to supply the argument that was missing in Quinn and Broome. I have offered a model of a reason-based desire, and suggested that this model repeats all the way down, so that we can in general understand desire as a response to a perceived reason. What Humeans have to do, in reply, is to show that this model always gives out at the last minute. (It must be 'always', because of their conception of the relation between desires and reasons.)

It may still seem that I have done no more than what Broome and Quinn did, i.e. assert baldly that if a desire to ϕ gives us no reason to ϕ, it can give us no reason to do those acts that subserve ϕ-ing. But there is an important difference between my strategy and theirs. They are attempting to refute Humeanism in its own terms, i.e. to use one of its two main claims to refute the other. I do not myself suppose that this can be done. I am trying to establish that Humeanism is false from premises with which Humeans may not agree, premises to do with the relation between desires and conceptions of value. The fact that Humeans can consistently reject my argument is neither here nor there. In essence, the difference between my argument and the Broome–Quinn attempt is that they argue:

> Because a desire for ϕ-ing gives us no reason to ϕ, it gives us no reason to do what subserves it.

I argue:

> Desires are held for reasons, which they can transmit but to which they cannot add. Therefore a desire for which there is no reason cannot create a reason to do what would subserve it.[6]

It would be nice, of course, to have an internal refutation of Humeanism—or at least something that would enable me to claim some advantage in terms that Humeans could not consistently reject. A final suggestion here, the seeds of which I owe to Brad Hooker, is that on the Humean showing we have as much reason to abandon a desire which there is no reason to have, as to do what will subserve it. For Humeans, since there is no reason to have this desire, there can be no reason not to abandon it.[7] Abandoning it must then be rationally permissible. But if this is so, there can be no reason to do what subserves it, for if we had a reason to do what subserves the desire, and no reason to abandon the desire, abandoning it would not be rationally permissible.

I now turn to consider some difficulties for the position I have outlined. The first difficulty is about tie-breakers. Might it not be the case that, where we have equal reasons on either side, or the reasons on either side are incommensurable, a desire to do one rather than the other can decide the issue, i.e. resolve the dilemma, and that it does so by acting as a reason over and above those that contributed to the situation to be resolved? Raz and Scanlon both allow that there are such cases.[8] It is certainly the case that a desire for one rather than the other might itself explain why that was what actually got done. But that is a motivational matter. Can we say that the desire acts as a good reason in such a case? The argument for saying so is that it would be irrational of someone who took it that the reasons on each side were equally strong, but who wanted one more than the other, to do the other. But it does not seem promising to claim that though desires can be reasons, they can only achieve this normative status in this sort of tie-breaking situation. One might say that any reason can resolve a tie if one leaves it until last, and wheels it in only once the tie has been created.

---

[6] I am grateful to Joseph Raz for helpful discussion on this point.

[7] This may not be true once the desire is well entrenched, since we will by then probably have committed resources to it, which might alter the equation by giving us a reason to carry on so as not to waste the resources committed.

[8] See Scanlon (1999: 47–8); Quinn (1993a: 246–7); Raz (1986: 142); also Bond (1983: 16–18).

Returning to the claim that it would be irrational of someone who took it that the reasons on each side were equally strong, but who wanted one more than the other, to do the other: are we so sure that this is the case? It is true that it would be very odd of someone who very much preferred ϕ-ing to ψ-ing still to ψ when the reasons were equally strong on either side. (Preferring ϕ-ing to ψ-ing counts here as desiring to ϕ more than one desires to ψ.) But the question to be asked is whether this description of the situation is coherent in the first place. How can it be that the agent much prefers ϕ-ing to ψ-ing when he does not think of ϕ-ing as in any way better than ψ-ing? What is odd is preferring ϕ-ing to ψ-ing at all in that situation, not subsequently thinking of that preference as a reason in favour of one decision rather than the other.

The second difficulty stems from thoughts about the desires of others rather than those of the agent. There is strong pressure to allow that someone else's desires can themselves be a reason for me to act in one way rather than another. And it would be very unattractive to say that the desires of others can be reasons for me when my own desires cannot. We must allow, then, that the desires of the agent can be reasons, or give the agent reasons. Is this not the end of the debate? No, in two ways.

First, we should think twice before allowing that the mere fact that someone else wants something gives us any reason at all. It might be that such desires only pass on reasons rather than creating them. That is, if there is some reason for them to want what they want, we have some reason to help them get it. But if there is no reason for them to want it, their wanting it creates no reasons for us any more than it does for them.

Second, the DBR theorist wants the desires of the agent to play a role that the desires of others cannot play. But even if a desire of hers does in some way give me a reason, a desire of my own can only give me reasons in the same sort of way[9]—probably by virtue of the prospect of some good, for her or for me or for someone else. The most obvious goods in the offing are those to do with satisfaction, disappointment, frustration, and contentment—the good

---

[9] Not necessarily exactly the same way. Michael Lacewing pointed out to me that the desires of others may generate reasons for me partly in virtue of considerations of autonomy, which are hardly at issue in my own case. And there may be other differences too. But I maintain that they will not be the right sort of difference for the Humean.

and bad aspects of achieving or failing to achieve or get what one desires. In this sense, a desire can indeed be a reason, or at least we can say that the presence of the desire affects the balance of normative reasons that we have, since it opens up the prospect of deriving some satisfaction from achieving the thing desired. But as such it is functioning just like any other practically relevant consideration. And what is so functioning is not itself necessarily a desire of the agent's.

One might think that there are features of the way in which the desires of the agent generate reasons that distinguish it from the way in which the desires of others do so. Perhaps thoughts about one's own frustration and disappointment play a different role from thoughts about the frustration and disappointment of others. But even if we admitted this, it would not give DBR theorists what they want. What they want is a picture in which the desires of the agent are essentially involved in every possible reason, and that they do this by converting what is not an end in itself into an end for that agent. What we have now reached is nothing like that. All sorts of things are now in the reason-grounding business, and the desires of the agent are really playing no special role at all of the sort suggested. This is why we can admit that if the agent has some desire, this will make a difference to the reasons he has. We can admit this because the way in which the desire makes a difference is not the way suggested by the DBR theorist.

So there is no danger that our admission will re-establish the DBR thesis, for two reasons. First, even if all desires do ground reasons for the desirer, this does nothing to show that all reasons are similarly grounded. Second, the way in which the desire-grounded reasons are grounded is not the way that Humeans need, since those desires ground reasons for others as much as for the desirer.

We might think it significant that in some sense the desires of the agent are always reasons for that agent, even if they are only reasons because they raise the prospect of satisfaction and of frustration. For in our own case this just takes us back to other desires of ours, desires for contentment and satisfaction, aversions to disappointment and to frustration, which is just the sort of place that the DBR theorists want us to end up in. But this is a mistake. It is true enough that we do not want to be disappointed or frustrated, and that we do desire the contentment that often comes with achievement. But we desire contentment for a reason, namely what it is like to be contented, just as we are averse to disappointment because of what it is like to be disappointed. What is true is that we don't dislike disappointment for a *further* reason, one that lies beyond the nature of the thing we dislike. But this does nothing to show that we do not dislike disappointment for a reason, nor that other people's dislike of disappointment functions as a reason for us in a way different from our own, which is what would be needed for this defence of desire-based reasons.

This is just further evidence of the general truth that everything we desire, we desire for a reason (except for the pathological urge). That reason will either be those features of the thing desired for which we desire it, or features of other things to which this is related. If we desire the thing for such a reason, the object of our desire is presented to us *sub specie boni*, that is, as a good.

There remains an awkward point to deal with, the advice point. Can we find any way of allowing that someone's having a certain aim gives him reasons that he would not otherwise have, without allowing that desires at least add to the store of reasons, even if they are not the only source of them? The original problem was that in giving advice to someone we might announce that we see no reason whatever to adopt the aim he has adopted, but that given that he has adopted that aim, there is one way of pursuing it which is so much more likely to be effective than any others that he would be irrational not to take it.

There is a way out of this difficulty. The adviser's point is that it would be irrational, having adopted this aim, not to take this method (call it way w) of pursuing it. Rationality requires, we might say, that those with this aim pursue it in way w, even though it does not require us to have this aim. Now one way of hearing this sort of remark is as saying that rationality requires of us that we either abandon this aim or pursue it in way w. There are, we see, two ways of doing what rationality requires here, not just one. And this seems to show that what rationality requires of us is one of two complexes: either we have this aim and pursue it in way w, or we do not act in way w and abandon the aim.

We do say, as in giving advice, that though your project is totally irrational, still if you are going to pursue it, this way is much more sensible than that one. But this need not mean that your adoption of this project renders some ways of pursuing it more rational than others. Suppose, for instance, that your project is the utterly irrational one of subverting your own projects, and that we advise you to pursue this project in way *w*. We can use distinctions that will play a more significant role in the next chapter, thinking of this remark as a remark about [how to act if one has this project]. Rationality requires that [those with this irrational project should pursue it in this way rather than that, or else abandon it]. In hearing things in this way, we are taking it that the supposed conclusion that for such people this way of acting is more rational than that cannot be detached from what we already have. That way of acting is not rendered more rational than it would otherwise have been by the fact that rationality requires those with an irrational project to act in that way. It remains irrational to act in that way. What rationality enjoins is one combination rather than another: having this project and acting in this way as against having this project and acting in some other way. It enjoins this without enjoining that those with the project act in this way; it achieves this feat by refusing to enjoin or even to permit the project.

The question then is whether we can 'detach' a certain conclusion from certain premisses. The argument concerned is:

You ought, if *e* is your end, to pursue *e* in way *w*.
e is your end.
So you ought to pursue *e* in way *w*.

Is this argument valid or is it not? The advice point hangs on taking it to be valid, since the conclusion amounts to the advice we are supposed to be giving. And for the moment the answer to the advice point lies in insisting that no such conclusion can be detached.

APPENDIX
Korsgaard on Instrumental Reason

Korsgaard argues that what she calls the 'instrumental principle' (IP) cannot be the only rational principle. The IP 'requires us to take the means to our ends'. Korsgaard glosses this right at the outset of her discussion (1997: 215—all further references in this Appendix are to this paper) as 'if doing a certain action is necessary for or even just promotes a person's aims, the person obviously has at least a prima-facie reason to do it'. We will find reasons, however, to doubt whether this gloss in terms of the prima facie can be the core of the IP.

Korsgaard's tactic is to try to show that the IP cannot stand alone as a normative principle. We need a normative, not a factual, conception of an end if we are to make room for the possibility of people both having an end and failing to pursue it—both having it and failing to take (appropriate) means to it, that is. In the absence of that possibility, it is impossible for anyone to break the IP—but in that case the IP cannot stand as a normative requirement or guide. The instruction 'stay on the path' has no normative content if nothing would count as leaving the path. But, Korsgaard tells us, every practical reason must be both a motive and a guide (p. 219), and since the IP fails this test, it cannot have normative status.

It has never been clear to me what Korsgaard means by a motive. But we can leave any such worry aside, for the crucial point turns only on the notion of a guide: the IP cannot act as a guide because one cannot fail to follow it. The argument for this conclusion is on p. 229. Suppose that someone acts in the sort of way that we would normally call failing to take any means to their ends. Still, as Hume understands the IP, such a person has not really broken the IP at all. For, as Hume sees it, the IP requires only that we take the means to the ends that we are *going* to pursue, and we cannot fail to do this. 'Whatever you do is the means to the end you are *going* to pursue. . . . How can you be guided by a principle when anything you do counts as following it?'

Our response to this must surely be to question whether the IP must, for Hume, be what Korsgaard says it must be. We find our answer on p. 223:

> If the IP is the only principle of practical reason, then to say that something is your end is not to say that you have a reason to pursue it, but at most to say that you are *going* to pursue it (perhaps inspired by desire). . . . the IP instructs us to derive a reason from what we are *going* to do.

But here we will want to say, I suppose, that the IP should, in Hume's hands, be directly expressed in terms of desire, so that the beginning of the quotation above should read, 'If the IP is the only principle of practical reason, then to say that something is your end is not to say that you have a reason to pursue it, but at most to say that you *want* to pursue it.' Why has Korsgaard taken it upon herself to write otherwise? The answer lies in her claim that 'Hume identifies a person's *end* with what he *wants most*, and the criterion of what he wants most appears to be what he actually *does*' (p. 230). But this, as we will see, strays in the way in which it supposes that a person can only have one end, and in the consequent way in which it introduces talk, not of what a person wants, but of what he wants most.

We should distinguish between two principles of practical rationality, as Korsgaard does right at the beginning of her paper. The first is our old friend IP, and the second is the 'principle of prudence' (PP). The latter is the requirement that we act in the light of our own 'overall good'. Like Korsgaard, I understand this as a principle of balance: it requires of us a certain balance (or imbalance) between our various ends (and the means available for us to pursue those ends). She writes,

> This principle concerns the way in which we harmonize the pursuit of our various ends. Its correct formulation . . . is a matter of controversy. . . . The common element in all of these formulations is that they serve to remind us that we characteristically have more than one aim, and that rationality requires us to take this into account when we deliberate. We should deliberate not only about how to realize the aim that occupies us right now, but also about how doing so will affect the possibility of realizing our other aims. (pp. 216–17)

The IP, as a principle, could apply to a single end, one would have thought. By contrast, the PP only enters the ring when one has more than one end. Of course, the IP still applies when one has more than one end—but it applies to each end severally. It says, of each end that one has, that one should adopt means to that end (according to Korsgaard, anyway). It says nothing about which of one's ends is or should be paramount; that is, as addressed to each end individually the IP says nothing, and need say nothing, about 'what one most wants'. Such considerations are the province of the PP, if of either principle. But in fact the PP need not say anything about 'what one most wants'. It could be indifferent to actual strength of desire. For it might tell us to pursue an end other than the one we most want to pursue at the moment.

If it does such a thing, is the PP a principle that the Humean can accept at all? I am tempted to think that it is. There might seem to be an easy way of showing that it is, which is by supposing that we all have an 'overall end' of the harmonizing sort. This is just a further desire, whose object is a certain balance of satisfactions of other desires. But if we conceive of the PP in this way, we render it incapable of doing the job required of it. One way of conceiving of that job is as that of preventing us from pursuing always the end we most want to pursue at the time. But if the end of harmonizing is just another end that is thrown into the ring with the others that it is supposed somehow to regulate, it will be inefficacious unless it is the strongest desire. But it is impossible for reason to demand that the end of harmonization be the strongest end.

My own view is that Humeanism should allow the PP as a further

rational principle in addition to the IP, but not as specifying a further end
that we ought to have (a rationally required desire). The basis for this view
is that the real battle is between the Humean claim that all our individual
ends are determined by desire rather than by reason and the 'rationalist'
view that some at least are determined by reason. In *this* battle it does not
matter, directly, what one thinks about ways of harmonizing one's pursuit
of one's ends. Of course, it may turn out that there is no way for the
Humean consistently to allow the existence of the PP as a rational principle, in addition to the IP, and if so, this will constitute an independent argument against Humeanism. For the balancing of our aims against each other
would then have to be merely a matter of which one we most strongly
desire at the time of action, which I see as a deeply unsatisfactory
situation.

So I take it that we should be careful to distinguish the role of the IP
from that of the PP. What then, considered as addressing individual ends,
should we take the IP to be saying? Does it require of us that we adopt
means to each of our ends? (Call this IP^a.) Surely not. There is a distinction between having an end and pursuing that end—a distinction that
Korsgaard systematically ignores. At least, there is such a distinction if to
pursue an end is to take steps to achieve it, rather than just to have it as
an end. (The ambiguity of the phrase 'pursue an end' may be part of the
problem here.) For we may have many ends that we take no steps to
achieve, for all sorts of good reasons. Perhaps, though we genuinely want
to achieve this, and would set ourselves to do so if we had more time or
some spare resources, still at the moment we do not have enough of either.
It seems just wrong to say that if we are not taking steps towards achieving it, it is not one of our ends. One of my ends is to recover my earlier
skill on the double-bass. I am doing nothing about this at the moment,
because I am just too busy trying to finish this book in every spare moment.
But though this might make us suspicious of my sincerity, it is far from
absolute proof that my profession of this end is either insincere or even
merely mistaken.

The second thing that IP could be saying (IP^b) is that for each of one's
ends, one has some reason to take steps in pursuit of that end. As we saw,
in her second sentence Korsgaard wrote, 'if doing a certain action is necessary for or even just promotes a person's aims, the person obviously has
at least a prima-facie reason to do it'. So does the IP just say that we have
a prima facie reason to take steps in pursuit of each of our ends?[10] If so,
what would even count as an action in breach of the IP? Presumably we

[10] Note that the PP is definitely not a prima facie principle. It is not that we have
some reason to pursue our overall good, though we might have more reason to do
something else. This casts doubt on Korsgaard's initial reading of the IP in prima
facie terms.

would have to wait until we had no other end, and then, if we did nothing in pursuit of this end, it would be established that we had not done what the IP told us to. This is all rather peculiar, and I leave it on one side for a moment.

The third thing that the IP could be telling us (IP^c) is that for each end, if we do in fact take steps to achieve that end, we should adopt the most effective ones available. I should confess that this is what I do suppose the IP to say. We are in breach of the IP, not when we fail to take steps to an end, which is often rationally defensible, but when we take steps that are (acknowledged to be) less effective than others available to us.[11]

I suppose, therefore, that IP^a is false. IP^b is peculiar, because it is not clear what it could be to flout a prima facie reason. I think the point could only be that if one has no other end, one's prima facie reason to take steps towards this end converts into an absolute reason. In this unusual situation the failure to take steps towards the end is proof positive that one does not really have the end. Here, then, there is a 'requirement' that one cannot fail to meet. But this does nothing to discredit the IP as a normative requirement. For IP^c is (or at least may be) true and floutable. Whenever I take the acknowledged less effective means to one of my ends, I act against a rational requirement, and so act irrationally.

I conclude that the following could all be true together, within the constraints of Hume's account:

(*a*) The IP is the only rational requirement.[12]
(*b*) I have end *e*.
(*c*) I am taking steps to this end.
(*d*) The steps I take are acknowledged less effective than others available to me.

This persuades me that Korsgaard's argument that the IP cannot be the only rational requirement is defective. One can be motivated by the recognition that this is the most effective means to one of one's ends, and one can also flout that fact in a way that is sufficient to establish one's

---

[11] Note that, on this understanding, if we were to have only one end, the second and third readings of the IP come to the same thing.

[12] In putting things this way I am ignoring the PP, and have said nothing here about Korsgaard's other argument, which is that Hume can have no notion of a rational requirement, since the only form of necessity that he allows is causal necessity. Even though I acknowledge that this is true, and hence that technically Hume cannot think of the IP as a rational requirement at all, I leave this matter aside. For my real interest is in the position inspired by Hume, though not available to Hume himself, that the IP is the only rational requirement: that desire converts something that is not an end in itself into an end for the desirer, and thereby gives the desirer reasons that he did not have before, reasons to do those actions that are the most effective means to that end.

One's first thought, however, is that we should simply allow that there are two ways in which an action can get to be what we ought to do: the objective way and the subjective way. According to OD, what makes it the case that he ought to have helped is an objective matter, that she was alone and in trouble. According to SD, what makes it the case that he should have offered help was that he thought she was alone and in trouble. Suppose he was quite wrong about that; this makes no difference, we might say, he should still have offered help. There was no (objective) reason to offer help, but he should have done so all the same.

I think that this idea that there are two quite distinct potential grounds for a duty is in the end untenable. Whatever the relation between features of the situation and potential action, that relation cannot also hold between the agent's beliefs and potential action. So if we do have these two distinct grounds for duties, there must be two distinct grounding relations: one that makes duties out of features of the situation, and the other that does it out of (possibly false) beliefs. Whatever it is that the agent's beliefs are capable of doing, it cannot be what states of affairs can do. So if there is a right-making relation that holds between states of affairs and actions, can there be a *second* such relation holding between beliefs and actions: a right-making relation, indeed, but a different one? The awkwardness of this suggestion is a strong incentive to find some way to do without it.

We need to be sure that we really would be dealing here with two distinct right-making relations. To do this, we should distinguish between two ways of understanding subjective duties. The first of these grounds subjective duties in what the agent believes. The second grounds them in such states of affairs as 'that the agent believes that p'. There is a considerable difference between these, at least at first sight. For the second view grounds these duties always in something that is the case, namely that the agent so believes, while the first view will sometimes ground duties in things that are not the case, where things are not as the agent believes. This tells us immediately that the first view really does require a distinct right-making relation, since it supposes (presumably) that the 'objective' relation only obtains between things that are the case, on the left, and potential actions on the right, while the 'subjective' one can make do with things that are not the case on the left. Matters look different with the second view, which requires the left-hand side of its 'subjective' relation to consist always of things that are the case, restricting this only to subjective matters of fact such as 'that the agent believes'. In this sense, there is not such a glaring difference between the two right-making relations, since both restrict their left-hand side to things that are the case. But we should remember the way in which our supposed subjective duties are generated. They are generated by asking what duties the agent would have had if things had been as he (defensibly) supposed. What the subjective view does is to turn potential duties, ones that the agent would have had if things had been different, into actual, but subjective, duties. And this contrast does seem stark enough to ground the claim that we must therefore be dealing with two distinct right-making relations.

But why is it incoherent to suppose that there are two distinct right-making relations operating in the same area? We might think that we are perfectly well used to dealing with distinct but competing right-makers, for we deal without difficulty with competing reasons for and against action in a particular case. Is the present situation any worse than that? Yes, it is. For the ordinary reasons for and against acting in a particular case all stand in the same sort of relation to the action proposed, either favouring it or not. But the suggestion I am opposing is that, as well as all this, there is another similar relation in which it is now the agent's beliefs that are either favouring the action or not. I think that this is one relation too many. Suppose that, on the first relation, the balance of considerations favour acting, while on the second they do not. How are we to come to an overall judgement about whether the proposed action is right or wrong? I don't mean to ask this question from the point of view of the agent, exactly: partly because, though the agent can see that there are these two relations, presumably, he is incapable of distinguishing between them in practice, since he cannot distinguish in practice between how the world is and how he takes it to be. The point is rather how *we* are to suppose that the demands of these two competing relations are to be put together. My own view is that once we conceive of the second relation as a relation of *demanding*, like the first, we lapse into incoherence. There cannot be two sorts of demand, an objective sort and a subjective sort.

But if this is right, we have an awkward choice to make. If there is only one sort of demand, which sort is it, objective or subjective?

There are considerable difficulties with either answer. For each answer has to explain away the appearances that support the other answer, and this is very hard to do.

It seems to me, however, blatantly obvious that most of our moral duties are grounded in features of the situation, not in our beliefs about how things are. It is because she is in trouble that I ought to help her, not because I think she is in trouble. What made it wrong for her to behave in this way was that she had promised not to, not that she believed she had promised not to. What made it wrong for him not to turn up was that it made it impossible for her to get home that evening. The reason why I should go and see my sister is that she has been ill. And so on. None the less, one may say, we do say things like SD. Believing that she has been ill, I should go and see her even if in fact I am quite wrong about that. Are there really no such duties as these?

Worried by this question we might try somehow to construct objective duties out of subjective ones. But this looks like a very difficult thing to do. After all, we can have objective duties without being aware of the features that ground them, even though we know perfectly well what we believe. The ignorance is an ignorance of matter of fact. Subjective duties are quite unlike this, in a recalcitrant way. (This point requires a qualification which it will shortly receive.)

So I turn to consider how one might defend the view that all duties are objective. One attractive route is sadly unavailable. Remember the understanding of subjective duties that I gave earlier, as those duties that we would have if our defensible beliefs were true. We could try to treat this as a definition of 'subjective duty', so that our subjective duties are defined in terms of objective duty. A subjective duty, defined in this way, is a duty that one does not have but would have if things were as one believed them to be. But this way of putting things reveals just what is wrong with our manœuvre. The whole point about subjective duties is that they are *not* ones that we don't have but would have if things were as we take them to be. We are supposed actually to have those duties here and now, even though they are somehow grounded in our perhaps false beliefs. Our over-neat definition fails entirely to accommodate this point.

With this manœuvre exposed as useless, there seem to be three main options available to me as an objectivist here. The first is to try to understand claims such as SD as evaluative rather than as deontic. All genuine 'shoulds' are objective, and the thought that, believing that she was in trouble, he should have offered help is really not what it appears. It is more like a remark to the effect that a better person, believing this, would have offered help. We know that SD cannot be what it seems because there was, surely, no reason for him to offer help. How then can it be the case that he should have done so? All we can say is that he would have done well to do something that there was in fact no reason to do. So the thought that he should have offered help is really a remark whose main purport lies in evaluation of how well he acted rather than in specification of a duty (how he *should* have acted) which has no grounds in reality.

I think that there is something in this first option, and that we need to keep it on the table. I am much less keen on the second option, which is to appeal to some appropriate version of the distinction between act and agent. This cuts across the first option, for we could distinguish between our deontic and our evaluative assessments of the act (was it right, was it good?), and we can distinguish between our deontic and our evaluative assessments of the agent (was he right to do what he did, was it good of him to do what he did?). This option requires for a full treatment a complex discussion of the act–agent distinction, which would not be appropriate here. The most obvious way, however, to use the act–agent distinction is to suppose that the objective side of things is somehow concerned with the act, while the subjective side is more addressed to the agent. I reject this contrast as misconceived, since I do not think that we can make sense of there being two requirements, one on the act (get yourself done), and one on the agent (do this thing). But I will not pursue the point here.[1]

The third option is more complicated, though I think that it is in its own nature clearer. (The first suffers from the obscurity of the distinction between the deontic and the evaluative, the second from the vicissitudes of the act–agent distinction.) This third option consists in the suggestion that SD does not specify a subjective duty at all, despite appearances. Instead, it specifies an objective duty, but one which governs combinations of beliefs and actions. Instead of

---

[1] I consider these issues in greater detail in Dancy (2001), and distinguish four versions of the act–agent distinction in Dancy (1993: 248–9).

understanding SD as saying that he had a duty grounded in his
beliefs about the situation, we may understand it as saying that he
had the objective duty that we all have of offering help when we
suppose someone to be in trouble. What we ought to do, on this
approach, is: offer help where we suppose help to be needed. The
grounds for this complex duty do not consist in our supposing help
to be needed, but in something else altogether.

The idea, then, is that there are simple objective duties and
complex objective duties, but no subjective duties. Some of the
complex ones consist in required or banned combinations of beliefs
and actions. A good example of this is the duty not to be what we
might call 'hypocritical'. I use this term to refer to the duty not to
believe that it is wrong for others to do this sort of thing while doing
it ourselves. This duty does seem to me to consist in a ban on a
certain combination. We should either believe it wrong for others
and not do it ourselves, or do it ourselves and not believe it wrong
for others. Neither of these combinations is itself required, of
course, but one combination, that of doing it ourselves while believing it wrong for others, is ruled out.

It is natural to say at this point that though it is indeed wrong to
do what one believes it wrong for others to do, and though this is
indeed a complex duty in the sense suggested, it can be converted
into a simple duty grounded in beliefs. For suppose that I should
not believe that it is wrong for others to do this sort of thing while
doing it myself, and that I do believe it wrong of others to do this
sort of thing. We immediately conclude that I should not behave in
that way myself, and this 'should' looks like a subjective 'should',
since its ground seems to be my having certain beliefs. But there is
a reply available to the objectivist here. The objectivist can try to
argue that my action is not made wrong by my believing it wrong
for others to behave in this way. My action may itself be entirely
innocuous—morally indifferent, that is. Or if the action were
made wrong by the belief, so is the belief made wrong by the action.
It is as true that I do wrong to believe that others should not behave
in this way when I propose so blithely to behave in that way
myself, as it is that I do wrong in behaving that way myself when
I believe that others should not. The inference, if there is such
an inference to be drawn at all, goes both ways with equal facility.
And what this shows is that the prohibition is really on the
combination of belief and action, and does not pass either to the

action itself, if one only believes, nor to the belief itself, if one only acts.

The suggestion here is that there is a logical manœuvre which the subjectivist has taken to be sound, which is commonly called 'detachment'. It involves starting from a complex requirement, that is to say, a requirement on a complex, and supposing that the requirement passes to part of that complex once the other part obtains. The obvious example of detachment involves the move from 'You ought, if you have promised, to keep your promise' via 'You did promise' to 'You ought to keep your promise'. In the case of hypocrisy, the move was from 'You ought, if you believe that others should not do this, not to do it yourself' and 'You do believe that others should not do this' to 'You ought not to do it yourself'.

What the objectivist is trying to combat, in defence of the view that all duties are objective duties, is the thought that remarks about how we should behave if we have certain beliefs convert into duties grounded in beliefs. There is, admittedly, a certain artificiality in this form of objectivist defence. But if we are to make sense of the relation between OD and SD without allowing the existence of two distinct right-making relations, this may be the cost that we will have to pay.

It is compatible with this objectivist position to allow that some of our duties are grounded in the beliefs of others. If someone believes her son to have been lost at sea, that belief alone is enough to give us a duty, say, to go and support her—or at the least not to make jokes in her presence about the horrors of a watery death. These duties are objective duties, because they are not generated by asking what duties we would have if the relevant beliefs were in fact correct. The way in which it is made wrong to make these jokes has nothing to do with whether the mother's beliefs are true or false. It might even be the case that beliefs of my own can ground moral reasons for me, if not duties exactly. Suppose that I have duties of self-preservation, and duties to care for myself. Believing as I do that I am utterly insignificant and worthless, I have (perhaps) a self-regarding duty to seek psychiatric help. But this again is an objective duty, grounded in a belief of mine conceived of as a state of affairs. It would be a subjective duty if, believing that I am utterly insignificant and worthless, I had a duty to abase myself before all and sundry. For to take things in this way is to take them as they would be if my beliefs were true, which is of course the approach that underlies subjective reasons.

There are, then, two main manœuvres that the objectivist might make in trying to allow that some remarks of the form of SD are true while disallowing the existence of duties grounded in beliefs of the agent rather than in features of the situation. The first of these involves appeal to the difference between the deontic and the evaluative; the second is the ban on detachment. The question, then, is what is the relation between these two manœuvres. Could one operate both at once, or must one make a choice, once and for all? I put this question aside, however, to answer later.

In his paper 'Duty and Ignorance of Fact' (1932), H. A. Prichard produces a series of arguments against objective reasons. The one that seems to me most effective is as follows:

> Consider, e.g., our attitude to the question: 'Ought we to stop, or at least slow down, in a car, before entering a main road?' If the objective view be right, (1) there will be a duty to slow down only if in fact there is traffic; (2) we shall be entitled only to think it likely—in varying degrees on different occasions—that we are bound to slow down; and (3) if afterwards we find no traffic, we ought to conclude that our opinion that we were bound to slow down was mistaken. (1932: 29)

The standard objectivist reply to this is that our duty not to drive straight out onto a main road is grounded in the chance that there be traffic on it, not in there actually being some. But Prichard responds to this that

> there are no such things as probabilities in nature. There cannot, e.g., be such a thing as the probability that someone has fainted, since either he has fainted or he has not. . . . The fact which we express . . . by the statement: 'X has probably fainted' . . . must consist in our mind's being in a certain state or condition. (ibid. 30)

How should an objectivist respond to this? One direct reply is to say that the duty to slow down is grounded in the fact that one does not know that there is no traffic. This does seem to me adequate to deal with Prichard's example.[2] There is, however, a further manœuvre available to the objectivist. This is to appeal to something that would have had to be brought in at some point, namely an agent-relative epistemic filter through which states of affairs or features

---

[2] I consider Prichard's arguments in much greater detail in Dancy (2001).

of the situation have to pass if they are to be allowed to stand as grounds for duties for a given individual.[3] Even if duties are always grounded in features of the situation, it might be that to serve as a ground a feature has to be one that, in some sense suitably devised, the agent is at least capable of discerning. It would obviously be too strong to claim that only those features that the agent has in fact noticed can stand as grounds for reasons for him. Wilfully closing one's eyes to the facts does nothing to diminish the number of one's duties. But equally features that I have no chance whatever of discerning are surely not capable of grounding duties for me. Suppose that, unknown and unknowable to me, someone has been buried alive in my garden during the night. Could this make it wrong of me to go away for a fortnight's holiday?

There are complications that beset this appeal to an epistemic filter. Obviously one question is how fine the filter is, i.e. what is meant by 'accessible to the agent'. Where do we want to draw the accessibility line on the scale between 'open to casual inspection' and 'literally impossible to find out'? But there need be no general answer to this, in my view. A further difficulty, related to the first, is revealed by an example of G. E. M. Anscombe's. While I sleep comfortably in my bed, someone leaves a newborn baby on my doorstep, and it dies during the night. In this case, I *could* have known that the baby was there. In a good sense, the fact was accessible to me. So does it pass the epistemic filter? The clue here is that it is not true that I *should have known*. I think that the Anscombe case shows that the filter is not purely epistemic. It has a normative aspect. The purpose of the filter is to prevent features of the situation from grounding duties for me. Features can do this if I am not at fault for not knowing them, and there are two ways in which that can come about. Either a feature is inaccessible (in whatever degree we give to that notion relative to the case at hand, but understanding it purely epistemically), or it is accessible but I am not at fault for failing to access it.[4]

We can combine these two manœuvres to deal with an example of Derek Parfit's, the general form of which he ascribes to Regan (1980). There is an explosion in a mine and 100 men trapped, and there are two shafts, with three floodgates, and water is rising in the

---

[3] I may have got this idea of an epistemic filter from Bergström (1996: 83).
[4] I was helped here by discussion at a class given by Philippa Foot and Anselm Müller in Oxford in 1998.

shafts. We suppose we know that all the men are in the same shaft, and that there is an equal chance of their all being in Shaft A and of their all being in Shaft B. If we close Gate 1, and they're in Shaft A, we save all 100; but if they're in Shaft B, they will all die. The reverse is true for Gate 2. If we close Gate 3, on the other hand, we will certainly save 90 of the men (for some reason or other to do with the way the gates work). The idea is that objectivists are committed to holding that closing Gate 1 has a one in two chance of being right, as has closing Gate 2. Closing Gate 3 is certain to be objectively wrong, since, if we knew the full facts, we would know whether, to save all the men, we should close Gate 1 or Gate 2. But the objectivists are wrong, for it's surely clear that, given our limited information, what we should do is to close Gate 3. That will certainly save 90 men, whereas closing either of the other gates gives us an expected number of lives saved of only 50. (This is because the expected utility of an outcome is the prospective gain it offers multiplied by the probability of achieving it, i.e. in this case 100 lives × 0.5 = 50 lives.) My reply to this is that if we allow as a reason the fact that we do not know which of Gates 1 and 2 to close, the objectivist can escape Parfit's example; not knowing this, we should close Gate 3. Further, which shaft the men in the mine are trapped in is a fact that will not get through the epistemic filter, and so is not one that can count as a reason.

Parfit's example is intended mainly to cause trouble for objectivists of a certain stripe, namely those who suppose that the ground of duty is the totality of objective fact. The position I have been arguing for is less extreme than this. I can admit that there are various questions that can be asked using one and the same (objective) notion of duty—or of right or of wrong. One can ask what it would have been right to do relative to a certain body of facts, and that body may vary. We may ask our question relative to all the facts, to all the facts available to anyone, to all the facts available to the agent, or any other maybe arbitrarily limited set of facts. (For example, one can ask what it would be right to do if one took into account only financial considerations.) And in each case other than the first, we can also vary things by loosening or tightening what we are willing to think of as available.

These variations, one of which is the agent-related epistemic filter, do nothing to undermine the objectivist's sense that the grounds of our reasons consist in features of the situation. It may

seem that the imposition of this particular filter is an *ad hoc* device
to escape the difficulties of Parfit's example. But I think that the
filter can be given an independent rationale. Part of the sense of
the principle that 'ought' implies 'can' is that practical requirements
that bind agents must be ones that it is not impossible for those
agents to live up to—otherwise the requirements are, as we might
put it, shouting in the dark. A similar thought applies to the suggestion that some of the grounds for our reasons might be ones that
we are utterly incapable of discerning. The grounds for our reasons,
like the reasons themselves, must lie within our capacities for recognition, if they are to be capable of being practically relevant for
us. So on occasions a feature that would have made an action
wrong, if at all discernible, can only serve to make that action
regrettable as things stand.

I suppose, then, that these two subjectivist arguments can be
rebutted. So my overall position is this. Our intuitions in favour of
objective duties are so strong that we should be willing to accept a
fair degree of artificiality in attempts to defend them. Accusing the
subjectivist of the unsound inference called 'detachment' does look
artificial, but the price is worth paying.

Before turning to consider ordinary practical reasons, we could
check our results so far against a specially hard case, that of the
relation between our moral beliefs and our actions.[5] What are we
to make of claims such as that, since he himself thought it wrong,
he should not have done it? Here the issue is the relation not
between our ordinary beliefs and our moral duties, but between
our beliefs about our duties and our duties. We should, we are told,
follow our conscience. But this must not be taken to mean that our
moral beliefs about our own actions are always true, indeed infallible. (Our moral beliefs about the actions of others are of course
far from infallible.) What then does it mean? One way of understanding the situation is by appeal to detachment again. Perhaps
the right structure to assign to the thought that one ought not
to do what one thinks it wrong to do is that of a complex
prohibition—a prohibition on thinking an action wrong, but doing
it all the same. The idea again is that even where one does think
the action wrong, the prohibition does not pass to the right-hand
side of that complex. The action is not made wrong by one's

[5] For this question, see Dancy (1977) and Broome (1999).

thinking it to be wrong, even though the complex prohibition is sound and one does think the action wrong. This amounts to saying that we should not detach the disputed conclusion. I take this example to constitute some defence of the ban on detachment.

2. *Practical Reasons and Beliefs*

When we turn to ordinary practical reasons, the same issues assail us with even greater force. It is common to read that rationality requires an agent who has certain beliefs to act accordingly, even if things are not as he supposes. This is sometimes expressed by saying that there are two distinct questions to be raised:

(OR) Are there any reasons for him to do this?
(SR) Would it be rational for him to do this?[6]

OR is answered by saying what features of the situation favour doing the action. SR is answered from within the agent's perspective, irrespective of whether things really are as he takes them to be. There is a slight complication here, which we noticed in a slightly different form at the end of Chapter 1.4. Only rationally permissible aspects of the agent's perspective are allowed to count. If an agent has irrational beliefs, those beliefs are not able to make rational any actions done in their light. (The irrationality of a belief will normally be a matter of how it was formed, but there may be some beliefs that are irrational no matter how they are formed, such as that one does not exist, or that the future precedes the past.)

So it looks again as if there are two sorts of requirement— rational requirements, now, rather than moral ones. There are objective requirements laid on us by features of the situation, and subjective requirements laid on us by our own (rationally permissible) beliefs. Our question again is how to understand the relation between these two supposedly quite different sets of requirements.

As before, there are three possibilities. The first is that things are as they appear: there are indeed requirements of these two sorts. The second is that the supposedly subjective requirements are an illusion, and that all is objective. This is the position I will try to

[6] For an example, see Parfit (1997: 99).

support. The third is that it is the supposed objective requirements that are the illusion.

This last view, subjectivism in the theory of practical reasons, is already damaged to the extent that one accepts the position argued for in the previous section, that all moral reasons are objective. For with that in place we would be imposing an enormous rift on the body of our reasons, considered as a whole, if we announced that the moral ones are objective and the non-moral ones not. Since nobody knows how to distinguish the moral ones from the non-moral ones in the first place, it seems almost incredible that there should be this degree of difference between them. Indeed, it is hardly a difference of degree—more a difference of style.

Still, perhaps this is how things are. My first target, though, is the view that there are two distinct sets of rational requirements, the objective ones and the subjective ones. These are sometimes called requirements of reasons and requirements of rationality. Here I want to say, as before, that it seems to me inconceivable that there should be two distinct sets of 'rational' requirements governing the same action. The relation between the features of the situation and the action which they generate most reason to do cannot be the same as the relation between the beliefs of the agent and the action that is made 'most rational' by them. With two sets of grounds we need two distinct 'favouring' relations. And, again, this seems to me to be one relation too many. The problem is not that the agent will feel rationally torn; he won't, because as far as the agent can tell, the two requirements necessarily coincide. Still, there will, supposedly, be two distinct requirements on the agent, one objective and the other subjective, and we observers have to decide for ourselves which of the two he should fulfil. And there seems to be, in principle, no way of answering this question. The question answered by one set of requirements is not the question answered by the other, but there is only one question for the agent, namely 'What should I do here?' (which is not a theoretical problem because we can suppose that the two requirements must seem to coincide for the agent), and only one question for us as observers, namely, 'What should he do?' But if there is only one question, there cannot be two answers.

This forces us into the uncomfortable position of having to choose between a picture of rational requirements as uniformly objective and a picture of them as uniformly subjective. We face the same dilemma as we did in the case of moral reasons, and much of the debate we saw there will be played out again in the new arena. This time, however, our intuitions in favour of the objective stance may be weaker. Certainly there is far more pressure in favour of the subjective view. For we do often judge an agent as rational or irrational in acting as he did, not in the light of the facts, but according to *his* light on the situation. Believing as he did, we say, there was only one sensible thing for him to do. Perhaps things were not as he supposed; but his view was a reasonable one, not one ruled out by some canon of rationality, and if one does take that view, the only rational choice is the one that he made. If we have to choose between thinking well of what he did and thinking badly of it, from the point of view of rationality we will have to think well of it.

The objectivist has to make some sort of sense of this way of thinking, while still insisting that it is a mistake to suppose that rational requirements can be laid on someone by his view of the situation, rather than by how things in fact are. Again, there are two main manœuvres available. The first involves recasting the supposed 'internal' rational requirements in evaluative rather than deontic terms. There was not the reason for doing this that he supposed; still, though he did what there was no reason to do, our answer to the question how well he acted is not determined by that fact alone. In many ways we will think he did well, for given his (rationally permissible) beliefs he acted as a sensible person would have done. That is, he did the action which, had his reasonable beliefs been true, would have been the one recommended by the reasons available in the case. Naturally this affects our overall assessment of his action, but cannot change our view of the reasons present in the case, or our answer to the question which action those reasons recommended.

The second manœuvre is the by now predictable claim that the supposedly subjective reasons, the ones stemming from the agent's perspective, are really objective reasons, reasons requiring or forbidding certain complexes of beliefs and actions. There are objective reasons favouring certain actions, that is, and objective reasons favouring certain combinations over others. One ought, believing that there is a snake in one's sleeping-bag, not to get into it. It does not follow that, given that one does (even reasonably) believe that there is a snake in there, one ought not to get into the bag. There may be no reason not to get into the bag at all (the suspicious lump is in fact a hot-water bottle kindly supplied by one's mother), indeed, there may be every reason to get in and get warm. But we would hardly think much the worse of the agent who, drawing the defensible conclusion that there is a snake in there, needs more persuasion before he gets in.

A sort of check can be run on this, as we did in the moral case, by considering the case where the agent has explicit beliefs about what there is most reason to do. Should we say that, if he believes that there is most reason to do D, D is what he should do? To say this would be to make his belief infallible, and surely that would be a mistake. To avoid that mistake, we should suppose only that there is a rational prohibition against the combination of [believing that the reasons call for this but not doing it]. To prevent this from yielding a prohibition against failing to doing it, for those who believe that this is what there is most reason to do, we need the ban on detachment.

So we should not detach, according to the objectivist. What is the relation between thoughts about detaching and the distinction between the deontic and the evaluative? This is a question which arose earlier, and which we shelved for a while. But it needs an answer. Even if detaching is a fallacy, we still have to say something about the relation between obeying the simple rules of rationality, the ones that specify what the reasons require, and the complex ones that govern combinations of beliefs and actions. It is plainly the case that an agent may, through no fault of his own, find himself in a position in which he does have mistaken but reasonable beliefs. He ought, so believing, to do an action that the reasons do not recommend. That is (as the objectivist sees it), he ought either not to believe these things, or to act accordingly. He ought also not to do the action that the beliefs suggest, since the actual reasons in the case recommend otherwise. We have to put all this together into a coherent picture, though this does not mean that our picture needs to be absolutely smooth. In a case of this sort, there are fissures in reality, and those fissures should not be smoothed over in our picture of the situation.

We do not want, I think, to suppose that simple rational requirements govern actions, while complex ones govern agents, as if they were talking to different audiences. This removes the tension in the situation, when in fact we want to preserve that tension and capture it appropriately. It is not as if the reasons-requirement is a deontic matter, addressed to the action (get yourself done!) while the rational requirement is an evaluative one addressed to the agent (be a person of such and such a sort!). The audience is the same one both times.

It seems to me that we need to appeal to the deontic–evaluative distinction in order to find something not too damning to say about the agent who acts in good faith and with good intentions, in a case where that agent is misinformed through no fault of his own. Just saying that he did the wrong thing seems inadequate. We want to be able, not to diminish the sense that what he did was wrong, but to diminish our condemnation of him for having acted wrongly. Of course the complex objective requirement is one that he did satisfy, and that is already something. But he might satisfy that requirement even if he ought not to have believed as he did. Among those who fail the simple requirement, then, there are better and worse. The worse is the one who *merely* satisfies the complex objective requirement. The better might be one who both satisfies that requirement and believes irreproachably even though mistakenly. Deontic conceptions give out at this point, and we need the evaluative if we are to draw the relevant distinctions.

There is a sense, then, in which the agent who does what there is no (or insufficient) reason to do is one who faces an accusation in the court of rationality, an accusation to which he has no defence as such; he cannot defend himself for what he did, but he can defend himself for doing it. This is the sense in which we might want to say that the apparently subjective requirements (actually complex objective ones) are more evaluative than deontic. And that claim is in addition to, and indeed acts as a necessary supplement to, any thoughts about the sins of detachment.

So far, then, our position on rational requirements is directly analogous to the position we took on moral requirements. There are no subjective requirements of rationality, though there are objective requirements on combinations of beliefs and actions. On this showing, the beliefs of the agent do not act as the ground for rational requirements, nor as the ground for reasons. But now we meet a complication similar to one we saw earlier. Why isn't it the case that the beliefs of the agent can make a difference to whether an action is rational or not, when it is clear that the beliefs of others can do so? For instance, that I believe that p is a reason for me to put up my hand when all those who believe that *p* are asked to raise their hands. According to Danish law, I am told, everyone is obliged to report to the relevant authorities if they believe that someone is abusing or neglecting a child. One way to understand the law is that if you find yourself harbouring this belief, then you are under an obligation to act on it. In principle, you can be prosecuted if you have this belief, but fail to act, irrespective of whether your belief is true or even reasonable. That I believe that everyone is out to get me is a reason for me to seek professional help. Here we have a belief which, if it were true, would not be the reason that it is. If it were true, I would have a reason not to put myself into the hands of professionals, where I will be at my most vulnerable. It is genuinely the belief (the believ*ing*) that is the reason, not so much the thing believed. But this is no threat to the picture we have been developing. The believings that are here acting as the grounds of reasons are functioning as features of the situation, not as the perspective from which judgements about how to act are made. So we can allow these things without allowing that any practical reasons are belief-based in the sense that I have been trying to deny.

The next point is to reiterate what was said about moral reasons, in this new context. Here, as there, the features that are capable of making a difference to how it is rational to behave are not just any features; they must be ones that are in some suitable sense, which I leave to be determined, accessible to the agent. An action is not shown to be sensible by the mere fact that it would lead to the best outcome, any more than it is by other utterly unknown facts. It might be best for someone who would otherwise die painfully of cancer at the age of 65 to eat certain foods now, at age 30, rather than others. But it would be hard to say that the reasons require this of him. Again, however, I stress that this sort of restriction to information that is suitably available to the agent does not reintroduce the sort of relativity to the agent's beliefs that I have been trying to combat.

Consider the question which horse one has reason to bet on in a race.[7] If the answer to this question depends only on matters of fact, and not on probabilities, it must be that one has most reason to bet on the horse that will in fact win and no reason to bet on

---

[7] I owe this question to Frank Jackson.

any other horse at all. Nobody thinks that this is the case. But how can the objectivist avoid it? We avoid it by appeal to the epistemic filter that all reasons must pass. And this will give us part of our response to a certain picture that has many adherents, which I end by considering. This picture has it that there there are two genuinely different conceptions of rationality, and that it is worth calling one objective and the other subjective. The action that is objectively rational is the one that will in fact produce the most good. (This is analogous to the horse that will in fact win the race.) The action that is subjectively rational is the one that is most favoured in the interplay between the amounts of good promised by each alternative and the probabilities of obtaining those goods.[8] The reason why the latter is to be thought of as a conception of subjective rationality is that the probabilities we are dealing with are subjective probabilities, i.e. they are constituted by degrees to which the agent believes that the relevant outcome will occur. (As we saw earlier, Prichard said that such probabilities must 'consist in our mind's being in a certain state or condition'.) This being so, that the agent has those beliefs (to that degree) is part of what makes the action rational, and so we are supposedly dealing here with subjective reasons once more.

To make progress on this issue, I think it is helpful to start by considering the rationality of belief separately, and working from that to the rationality of action. With belief, it is often held that there is no available conception of objective rationality similar to that for rational action which I have just mentioned. Rationality of belief is to be understood as what it is rational to believe given where one now is, i.e. as requirements on moves from one set of credences to another. These transference rules are uncontestably objective, in the sense that whether they hold or not is a matter that is not determined from the perspective of the agent. An agent who holds false beliefs on the transference rules relevant to his present position is not thereby rendered rational when he comes to believe what he ought not to believe, given where he started from. However, it might seem that these objective transference rules still tell us that the agent's present beliefs (or credences) make it rational for him to move in one way from there, and not in another.

---

[8] I am very grateful to Frank Jackson for helping me to see the relevance of this position.

Supposedly, therefore, we have achieved a conception of subjective rationality of just the sort that I have been trying to combat, since my original target was the view that the agent's beliefs can render one action (here: belief) more rational than another.

Let us, however, remember my earlier discussion of what I called 'hypocrisy'. The point there was not just that the prohibition of hypocrisy is itself objective (just as are the transference rules of the probability calculus), but that in the nature of the case what is prohibited is a combination of beliefs and actions. In cases of objectionable hypocrisy, it is not that believing that the action is wrong for others makes it wrong to do it oneself, any more than doing it oneself makes it wrong to believe it wrong for others to do it. What is wrong is to [believe that others should not do it and then do it oneself]. Now we don't need to think of this point as restricted to combinations of beliefs and actions. The same thing applies to combining the belief that others should not do it with the belief that one may do it oneself. We can apply this result here, then, in the discussion of the transference rules. What they enjoin or prohibit are moves from one set of credences to another, i.e. temporally ordered combinations of beliefs. The earlier credences no more make the later ones rationally required than failing to adopt the later ones make the earlier ones forbidden.

There remains a question about prior probabilities. The transference rules tell us how to move from one set of credences (the prior ones) to another. How do we get started on this? There must be some set of credences that we begin with, as it were. (This is a regress argument, based on the thought that one cannot be told to move in some direction if one is not somewhere in the first place.) These credences are not themselves subject to the transference rules, in the nature of the case, since we have not moved to them from other credences. Still, we might say, there is more than one possible set of prior probabilities, and which set one adopts will make a difference to what we are rationally required to do thereafter. Isn't this a sense in which the beliefs of the agent make it rational to believe one thing rather than another?

The answer is no. Prior probabilities are no different in this respect from the others. If the only rational requirements are on moves from one set of credences to another, all we have is the situation outlined before, under which there are objective rationality requirements on temporally ordered combinations of credences. We still do not have the earlier credences making the later ones rational or irrational. (We cannot detach the conclusion.) If, on the other hand, there are rational constraints on acceptable prior probabilities, this is not something it is hard for us to capture. For such constraints will again be on combinations, probably, only this time on simultaneous combinations rather than on temporally ordered ones. And if there are constraints other than those derived from considerations of internal coherence, e.g. constraints deriving from external considerations, these too can be expressed in our objective mode. Yet again, there is no reason to think that we have here a case of a belief or set of credences making another belief rationally required or forbidden.

I now return to the issue of the rationality of action. What I have urged above is that even though we are conceiving of probabilities as subjective, in the sense that they are quotients of credences, this does no damage to our objectivizing approach to the requirements of rationality. The challenge that I was trying to deal with was the claim that there are indeed two conceptions of practical rationality, one that is worth calling objective and another that is worth calling subjective. The objective conception is that of the action that is in fact the most successful; the subjective one is that of the action whose expected utility is the greatest, which is a function of the amount of good promised and the probability of achieving that good. Probability here is to be understood as before, in terms of quotients of credences.

My response to this is that the first conception is not a conception of the rational act in any sense, but simply that of the successful, one might even say fortunate, act. The second conception is much more like a conception of rationality; but is it a case of an act that is made rational by certain beliefs of the agent, among other things, or is it another instance of a rational requirement on a combination, some part of which is a belief of the agent? Again it seems to me to be the latter. The complication here is that we have three players, the amount of good in prospect (which can be viewed as a matter of certainty for present purposes), the probability that we will achieve that good, and the action. The first of these, understood as certainty, is not itself a subject of rational requirement. Beyond that, however, it is as true that if you are not doing this action, you should not be assigning a high credence to the proposition that it will be successful as it is that if you do assign a high credence to that proposition, you should be doing the action. What is prohibited is combining either action and non-belief or inaction and belief.

If we understand the amount of good promised as itself a matter of credences rather than of fact, this does not change the situation in any relevant way.

There is a possible challenge to this picture, derived from the fact that we need to be able to assess how well an agent is doing whose information is incomplete. But assessing rationality relative to incomplete information does not require us to think that the rationality we are assessing is subjective in any damaging sense. For either we are here dealing with probabilities or we are not. If we are, the issue has already been dealt with; and if we are not, this means that there is a difference between judging that *p* on the basis of information known to be incomplete and changing one's degree of *p*-credence in the response to a limited set of credences. And there is no reason to suppose that this introduces any new difficulties. The requirement that one judge that *p* in the light of a limited range of facts is no less objective than the requirement that one judge one way or another, or act in one way rather than another, given the situation as a whole. The rationalizing relation is the same, and it has things of the same sort on the left-hand side, namely features of the situation, not beliefs of the agent. That the number of things appearing there is reduced is neither here nor there.

It is worth remembering in this connection that the fact that I do not know something can itself be a reason. Suppose that my information is limited, that I know this, and that I have no time to make further enquiries. The action I have most reason to do might not be the one that I would have had most reason to do if I had had time to find out more of what I needed to know. This should remind us of Prichard's example of slowing down at a junction. In that case, the objectivist seemed perfectly able to say that the main reason for slowing down is that one does not know whether any traffic is coming. If one had known that there was no traffic coming, perhaps one would have had no reason to slow down.

I end this section with a summary. As in the moral case, we started from the view that some of our reasons are given us by features of the situation rather than by our beliefs. This left us initially supposing that we were dealing with two sorts of way in which an action could be 'rationalized', the first being by states of affairs, by things being this way rather than that, and the second being by the way the agent took them to be. But since these do not seem to involve the same notion of a rational requirement, and since there seemed to be no room for two distinct 'rationalizing' relations, we were led to suppose that all that is at issue when a belief appears to rationalize an action is that the agent defensibly believes something which, if true, would rationalize the action. We were, however, still able to allow a sense in which certain combinations of beliefs and actions (or just of beliefs) are rationally required or forbidden without this meaning that the beliefs make the action rational or irrational. It emerges, then, that there is no sense in which actions are rationalized, made rational, by beliefs of the agent. Since we have already established the same result for desires as for beliefs, we can conclude that there is no sense in which actions are rationalized, made rational, by psychological states of the agent.

So the two cases, that of ordinary practical rationality and that of morality, do go in parallel. There seems to be only one sense of 'rationally requires that' or 'makes rational', and only one of 'morally requires that' or 'makes right'. There is only one notion of a requirement of rationality, and only one of what morality requires of us. To the extent that we allow that there are such things as 'internal' or 'subjective' requirements of rationality, moral or practical, we understand these as things that would be required of us if our non-culpably false beliefs were in fact true, or as what it would be right or rational to do or believe on limited information.

APPENDIX
On Detaching

I have argued above that we do better to deny what is technically called detachability.[9] In this comparatively formal Appendix I discuss three questions. The first is whether there is really so great a difference between forbidding detachment and allowing it. The second question is why it is so important to deny detachment in the first place. The third is why it is so important to insist that this inference is not *formally* valid.

[9] For issues concerning detachment, see Chisholm (1963); Greenspan (1975).

Those who deny detachment (the 'non-detachers') will tend to say that you should ensure that if you have promised, you keep your promise; but that it does not follow that if you have promised, you should ensure that you keep your promise. By this they mean not only that it does not follow 'logically', but that it does not follow at all, because the relevant requirement is a requirement on a combination (promising and keeping one's promise) and does not pass to the action promised. The detachers, on their side, claim that if you have promised, you should (ensure that you) keep your promise. They point out that we have something normative to say to the person who has promised and is now considering whether to do what they promised to do. We can say 'You should do it because you promised'. The non-detachers do not deny this, exactly, so much as recast it. They say that what you should not do is to make a promise and break it. Now that you have made the promise, the only way you can do what you ought to do is to keep the promise. But this does not show that the conclusion 'You ought to do what you promised to do' is detachable.

The slightness of the difference here between detachers and non-detachers, with respect to a given case, is revealing. One party says that the situation is to be described in a way that hardly differs from the way preferred by the other party. There is not much gap between saying that you ought, if you have promised, to keep your promise and saying that if you have promised, you ought to keep your promise. If this is all that is at issue, the reason for saying one thing rather than the other is not likely to be a clear perception of any great difference between the two claims. In fact, the slightness of the difference is itself an advantage to the detachers. They are the ones, after all, who say that one can move easily from one way of describing the situation to the other. So in this respect the onus of proof lies on the non-detachers.

Non-detachers face another problem as well. They have said that the requirement to keep one's promise is a requirement on a combination (promising and keeping one's promise) and does not pass to the action promised. But they may admit that there are other requirements on combinations that do pass in this way. For instance, you ought, if unavoidably delayed, to ring up and warn your hosts if you can. You have been unavoidably delayed. So you ought to ring up your hosts and tell them so. The requirement on a certain combination of being delayed and alerting one's hosts passes to the action of alerting one's hosts. Non-detachers may admit that all requirements that depend in this sort of way on circumstances can be expressed conditionally, and all can be detached. What is the difference, then, between those that can be detached and those that cannot?

The matter can be expressed in formal terms as follows, where 'Ox' means 'x should ensure that', 'Dx' means 'x performs action D', and 'Bxp' means 'x believes that p'. Non-detachers find themselves saying that there are some cases in which we can move (in a way that is not formally valid, perhaps) from $Ox(p \rightarrow Dx)$ to $(p \rightarrow OxDx)$, but there are others in which we cannot. I, for instance, given what I have argued in the present chapter, need to say why we can *never* move from $Ox(Bxp \rightarrow Dx)$ to $(Bxp \rightarrow OxDx)$. Why is it that required combinations of belief and action never generate situations in which the believing requires the acting, though other required combinations do generate detached requirements?

Reasons for denying detachment come in three sorts. The first is the analogy with the well-known modal fallacy $(N(p \rightarrow q)$ & $p) \rightarrow Nq$, where 'N' stands for 'necessarily'. This is a fallacy because, though it is necessarily the case that if I have five pennies and you have three, I have more pennies than you do, it is not the case that if I have five pennies and you have three, it is a necessary truth that you have fewer pennies than I do. The suggestion is that a similar fallacy is involved in supposing that the inference $(O(p \rightarrow q)$ & $p) \rightarrow Oq$ is formally valid. I take this suggestion to be inconclusive in the present context. The question is whether the analogy is sound. The second sort of reason for denying detachment is that it can be directly shown to be invalid in the required range of cases. The third is that reasons derived from elsewhere put us into a position where we have to deny detachment, and the main question then is whether we can get away with it.

Offering reasons of the second sort, John Broome has recently produced counter-examples to detachability. For instance, suppose that I ought, if going to St Andrews, to get off the train at Leuchars; and suppose that I am going to St Andrews.[10] Then I ought to get off the train at Leuchars, if detachment is valid in this case. But, Broome asks, what if I ought not to be going to St Andrews? If so, I should not get off at Leuchars. The detached conclusion may be false even though the premisses from which it was detached are true. So detachment is invalid; it can take us from truths to falsehoods. Similarly, one might say, for promising. Let us allow that I ought, if I have promised, to keep my promise, and that I have promised. Ought I to keep my promise? Not if I ought not to have promised. An example might be a case in which I have promised to play someone a cheap trick. Since I ought not to have promised this, my having so promised cannot make it morally right for me to do it. So, again, the conclusion is non-detachable.[11]

In my view, however, though Broome's argument works well for overall oughts, it fails for *pro tanto* ones, which are the ones that really matter. Take the case of promising. It might be that what I have promised to do

---

[10] To understand this example, one needs to know that the train station for St Andrews is in fact in Leuchars, a small village some miles away.

[11] The application to moral cases is mine. Broome only considers cases of ordinary practical reasoning. His discussion of these matters is in Broome (1997), (1999) and (forthcoming). Broome's basic point is to be found in Ross (1939: 47).

is not overall right, and so that I should not do it. But it does not follow from this that my having promised to do it does not give me *some* moral reason to do it that I did not have before. It might be that I ought not, overall, to be going to St Andrews. But it could still be the case that if I am going to St Andrews, this gives me *some* reason to get off at Leuchars, even though overall I have more reason to stay on the train until Dundee, where my wife is waiting for me. So if '*Ox*' is understood as specifying a *pro tanto* reason, as I do here understand it, Broome's argument does little or nothing to undermine the validity of the detachers' principle ($Ox(p \rightarrow Dx) \rightarrow (p \rightarrow OxDx)$).

Problems do arise for detachers when we consider the various operations on the required conditionals. Where '*Bx*' means '*x* does action *B*', $Ox(Dx \rightarrow Bx)$ entails $Ox(-Bx \rightarrow -Dx)$, which, if the detachers are right, entails $(-Bx \rightarrow Ox-Dx)$. So, missing out the intermediate stage, is it true that $Ox(Dx \rightarrow Bx)$ entails $(-Bx \rightarrow Ox-Dx)$? Probably not, even if '*Ox*' is understood as a *pro tanto* ought rather than an overall one.

My reason for writing '$Ox(p)$' to mean '*x* ought to ensure that *p*' was that it enabled me to have an 'ought' operator that governed a proposition, without purporting to make sense of the idea of a proposition that ought to be the case (even a proposition that concerns what someone is doing). But the reading I have given should not be too tendentious. The most tendentious aspect of it is the time reference of the 'ensure that'. If $Ox(p)$ reads '*x* ought *now* to ensure that *p*', we can give little sense to remarks of the form '$Ox(x$ did not borrow the money last week)'. But we can say that *x* ought not to have borrowed the money last week, even though *x* can do little about the matter now. We might need a distinction between '*x* ought now not to have borrowed the money then' and '*x* oughted then not to have borrowed the money then'. Which of these is at issue in a remark like 'If you are not going to pay the money back, you ought not to have borrowed it'? This remark cannot mean:

(1) If you are not now going to pay the money back, you ought now to ensure that you did not borrow it,

for this is senseless. Nor can it mean:

(2) If you are not now going to pay the money back, you oughted then not to have borrowed it.

For this seems to be false. There was, we may suppose, nothing wrong with borrowing it (either overall or *pro tanto*). What is wrong is borrowing it and not paying it back. But the detachers are, it seems to me, committed to the truth of either (1) or (2) above, as logical consequences of the agreed starting-point, i.e. that you ought, if you have borrowed the money, to pay it back. And here I discern a weakness. It is not true that if you are not now going to pay the money back, you ought then not to have borrowed it. But the detachers are more or less bound to say that this is true, as an instance of the inference pattern they accept, namely $(Ox(-Bx \rightarrow -Dx) \rightarrow (-Bx \rightarrow Ox-Dx))$.

This seems to me to establish that detachment is not formally valid. But it leaves us with the question whether it might not be informally valid in a discriminable range of cases. Before pursuing that, however, I want to return to the discussion of the sorts of reason there might be for denying detachability. I suggested three sorts of reason. Those of the third sort depend on there being significant issues elsewhere in philosophy that require the denial of detachment. The first of these is exactly the one discussed in the bulk of this chapter, namely the sense, if any, in which our reasons depend on our own beliefs. The extreme position that I have been defending on this issue requires me to reject detachment for a wide range of cases, that is, all those involving beliefs of the agent in a certain way. This is not an argument that detachment is invalid, merely an incentive. There is a further incentive, however, which concerns the issues discussed in Chapter 2. I attempted there to argue, following Raz, Quinn, and Scanlon, that a desire to do D gives us no reason to do B where doing B subserves doing D. But I was forced to admit that there is a certain pattern of advice-giving in which one says 'I think that there is no reason to adopt the aim you have adopted, but given that you have adopted it, the most sensible way to proceed is the following'. This is apparently to say that adopting an end that one has no reason to adopt can give one a reason that one did not have before, a reason to do B rather than some alternative C. But the denial of detachment gives us a way of proceeding here. For we could allow that one has a reason, having adopted this end, to pursue it in that way, but deny that once one has adopted this end, one has a reason to pursue it in that way. Indeed, this is surely what those who deny the DBR thesis are going to find themselves doing. So the rejection of detachment is part of the rejection of desire-based reasons as much as of that of belief-based reasons.

If this is what we are forced to say, can we get away with it? So far I have only argued that detachment is not formally valid. The proof was a proof by counter-example. It was similar to a point I made earlier in the present chapter, concerning hypocrisy. There I argued that though there was a *pro tanto* prohibition on combining the belief that others should not do it with doing it oneself (or with the belief that it was acceptable for one to do it oneself), this did not convert into a situation in which doing it oneself made it wrong to believe that others should not do it. What was wrong remained stubbornly the combination. Neither conjunct was wrong alone, and neither was rendered wrong by being combined with the other. The *pro tanto* moral prohibition is on combining two things that are not severally prohibited.

The question now is whether we can discover in the way in which detachment fails as a formal inference some reason for saying that *all* cases in which the required conditional involves a combination of belief and action are cases where we should not detach. And we will then have to ask whether similar reasons apply to combinations of desires (aims, purposes) and actions intended to satisfy those desires. In a way we have now made room for saying this by showing that detachment is not formally valid. But this is not, one might think, fully satisfying yet. For we are admitting (at least for the moment) the informal validity of detachment in many instances.

It would be possible to argue that we are not in control of our beliefs in the sort of way that we are of our actions, so that moral requirements on beliefs make little sense. This would not rule out requirements on combinations of beliefs and actions, such as those involved in the rejection of hypocrisy, but it would rule out any detached requirement on a belief. Since all requirements of the form $Ox(Bxp \rightarrow Dx)$ will, by contraposition and detachment, generate $Ox(-Bxp)$, we emerge with reason to deny detachment in any such case.

There are two weaknesses in this manœuvre. The first is that it is not clear that we are going to be able to say the same about detached requirements on desires. The second is that we may feel that even if we are not in control of our beliefs in the sort of way that we are in control of our actions, it is not as if we have no control at all. There does not need to be that sort of control for moral (or other rational) requirements to make sense.

In assessing this matter, we need to remember that there is a good sense in which we are often not in anything worth calling control of what we do. Often we work hard to achieve something, but achieving it requires the help and support of others, as well as a bit of luck; we are certainly not in a position to do these things at will, as we are with the movements of our fingers. But it makes perfect sense to say that some of the things that we cannot do at will are morally admirable achievements and others are morally prohibited. The question then becomes more subtle. Believing that *p* is not normally (if ever) something we can achieve at will. But the reasons why this is so seem to be different from those that apply to the sorts of action that require luck or the help and support of other people. Our subtler question is whether the difference is sufficient to prevent detachability where belief is concerned when it is not where action is concerned.

It may be possible to make progress in this sort of direction, but I think that there is an altogether easier way.

I have suggested that there is reason to deny the formal validity of detachment. The question I am at present trying to answer is how to distinguish those detachments that are informally valid from those that are not. I am committed to answering this question because I have allowed (pro tem) that some detachments are valid, even if not valid in virtue of their form. But I now want to suggest that detachment is never valid. We can never move from $(Ox(p \to Dx)$ & $p)$ to $OxDx$.

This may seem surprising. But in fact the argument I gave to the effect that detachment is not formally valid is unexpectedly strong. Any case where we start from $Ox(p \to Dx)$ and attempt to infer $(p \to OxDx)$ is liable to the sort of worry that we saw in the case of borrowing the money. $Ox(p \to Dx)$ entails $Ox(-Dx \to -p)$, tempting us to infer $(-Dx \to Ox-p)$ by detachment. But there is a good question whether such inferences make any sense. Suppose I say that

(a) You ought to ensure that if there is someone before you in deep trouble, you give a helping hand,

and infer that

(b) If there is someone before you in deep trouble, you ought to ensure that you give a helping hand.

In my view, though the conclusion (b) here may be true, it is not properly inferable from the premiss. For after all, (a) entails

(c) You ought to ensure that if you do not give a helping hand, there is not someone before you in deep trouble,

which, by detachment, gives us

(d) If you do not give a helping hand, you ought to ensure that there is not someone before you in deep trouble.

And this makes no sense. But there is no way of allowing an inference to (b) without allowing the inference to (d). It is both or neither.

The way out is to insist that where we have $(p \to OxDx)$, we do not necessarily have $Ox(p \to Dx)$. We have been tacitly supposing that where there are moral requirements on us that only hold in certain conditions, these requirements are properly specifiable in conditional form. But we have now seen a reason to be wary of this admission. It would be better to insist that such requirements be written as $(p \to OxDx)$ rather than as $(Ox(p \to Dx)$. For otherwise we commit ourselves to making sense of $Ox(-p)$ in every case of an action that is conditionally required, which is surely impossible. The way out of this is to deny detachment *tout court*. A principle of inference that is capable of taking us from truth to nonsense, whether formally or informally, is one that we are better off without. Requirements on conditionals should be understood as distinct from conditional requirements. This rescues non-detachers from the difficulty of saying why some detachments are valid and others not.

4

The Theory of Motivating States

The position so far is as follows. In the first chapter I outlined a number of distinctions. I then argued against the claim that all good reasons are grounded in psychological states of the agent, whether it be beliefs or desires. I now turn to consider the other context in which we speak of reasons, that of motivation, or of the reasons for which people do what they do. My question here is which form of psychologism in the theory of motivation is to be preferred. This question assumes that we are to understand the reasons that motivate us as motivating states of ourselves (i.e. that some form of psychologism is true). In terms of that assumption, I argue that all such states are cognitive states. Lurking behind all this, however, is the thought that we should not be thinking of the reasons that motivate us as psychological states of ourselves at all. I leave it to Chapter 5 to argue that much more contentious claim.

If I think that all forms of psychologism are in error, why am I bothering to argue that pure cognitivism is the best form of this error? The answer is that it is hard to perceive what I take eventually to be the truth of the matter if one remains wedded to Humean (or even Nagelian) forms of psychologism. We need to understand that the cognitive lies at the basis of motivation if we are to get into a position from which we can see that what motivates us is not a state of ourselves at all, but rather the nature of the situation. It is not our believing that things are so that motivates us, I shall eventually be saying, but rather what we believe, namely their being so, or that they are so. We have, that is, to look through the believings to the things believed if we are to find the real source of motivation.[1] But it is much easier to see that this is so, if one has put behind one the persistent temptation to think that desire plays some significant role in what motivates.

---

[1] As I suggested, without any supporting argument whatever, in Dancy (1993: 32).

1. *The Structure of a Complete Motivating State*

Humeanism

We have already seen the structure that Humeanism imputes to a complete motivating state. Its elements are two: a belief and a desire. The structure consists of a certain asymmetry. The role played by the belief is quite different from the role played by the desire, though each can only play its role when the other is there playing *its* role as well. What is more, the desire dominates in some way. There are two possible accounts of the nature of the asymmetry. The first simply appeals to the distinction between two directions of fit. The asymmetry just consists in the fact that the desire is a state with which the world must fit, and the belief is a state that must fit the world. The second account of the asymmetry appeals to a distinction in causal role. The shorthand for this is the claim that desires are active or ert while beliefs are inactive or passive or inert. Both forms of asymmetry give a good sense to the idea that the state playing the role of desire is the dominant partner.

The distinction between two directions of fit is well known.[2] In the present debate it is used to show that for there to be an intentional action the agent must be in two distinct states, one of which has one direction of fit and the other of which has the other. When these two states are brought together, as it were, action can occur; and this is presumably because motivation consists in the concurrence of the two states. It is not as if, when the two states come together, the agent will *also* be motivated to act in one way rather than another. Rather, motivation is explained by its constitution, not by laying out antecedent conditions for its occurrence.

The distinction between two causal roles is harder to manage. It is possible to exaggerate the degree to which belief must be seen as inert. It can be said, and has been said, that being inert, belief cannot cause anything at all. Belief contributes by its presence to the causal potential of the desire, but it has no causal powers of its own. This is not impossible. It may be that the belief–desire complex has causal powers that neither the belief nor the desire enjoy separately, but that those powers cannot be carved up into

---

[2] Anscombe (1957: 56); Smith (1987); Humberstone (1992); see also Ch. 1.5 above.

the separate causal contributions of belief and of desire. None the less, it seems to me that there is no reason for depriving belief of all causal power whatever.

At the back of one's mind here should be the Humean picture of practical rationality, under which reason is and should only be the slave of the passions, and it is impossible for a passion to be contrary to reason. Belief, we may say, finds out the means to ends set by desire. This is a genuine asymmetry of causal role (with desire dominant), but not one that requires us to think of belief as causally inert. Certainly there is very little reason to suppose that Hume himself thought of beliefs in that way. His mental economy is a causal economy in which belief, understood as a lively idea, plays a (causal) role that could not be played by less lively ideas, e.g. those of the imagination. And indeed his account of the causal relation, however eventually we understand it, is not one that makes it very attractive to assert that belief cannot stand in that relation to anything at all. The question then is where the view that belief is causally inert comes from, since it does not come from Hume.

Nagel

Nagel (1970, ch. 5) distinguished between motivating and moti-vated desires. Motivating desires are the ones that 'simply assail us'. But not all desires are like that. Many 'are *arrived at* by decision, and after deliberation' (p. 29). Such desires are explained by the beliefs in the light of which one comes to have them; for instance, the desire to take one's child away from the school she is attend-ing may be formed in the light of the belief that in another school she would have been much further ahead than she is. In cases like this, the belief leads, and the desire that is necessary if there is to be action follows. In similar vein, John McDowell (1978) suggested that one may desire not to do an action as a result of coming to believe that it would be wrong.

There are two questions left open by Nagel's distinction. The first is whether, in all cases where we arrive at a desire as a result of acquiring certain beliefs, the new desire is always eventually to be explained by the antecedent presence of a further desire. In the case of the unsatisfactory school above, one might reasonably suppose that one has an antecedent concern or desire that one's child be well educated. This more basic concern explains why we form the new desire to remove our child in the light of our new belief. But Nagel suggests that this need not always be the case. No doubt the Humean pattern is common, but it is not universal. Relevant here is the fact that Nagel slightly misrepresents the Humean view by characterizing unmotivated desires as ones that 'simply assail us'. My desire for my children's welfare is not a desire that 'simply assails' me, any more than is my desire to get a break from work at some point in the summer. That description should be kept for cases like the sudden desire to touch a woman's elbow or a yen for a cool beer, or perhaps for the peculiar desires that are said to assail pregnant women. It would be better, as Schueler suggests (1995: 21), simply to contrast motivated desires with desires that we do not arrive at after decision and deliberation. This gives us a suitably exhaustive distinction. But the effect of the change is greatly to increase the proportion of cases in which an action is to be explained by eventual appeal to an unmotivated desire.

The second question left open is the nature of the desire that we come to have in the light of our beliefs—what having that desire amounts to. One possibility is that all motivated desires are psychological states relevantly similar to urges or some other sorts of unmotivated desire. But Nagel suggests that though, if the agent is indeed motivated, we know that he has a relevant desire, what it is for the agent to have that desire is left open. That the agent has the relevant desire is, he says, a logically necessary condition for the belief to motivate, but 'not necessary either as a contributing influence, or as a causal condition' (1970: 30). This seems to mean that the motivated desire may not be an independent existence, in Humean terms; that is, it need not be a self-standing psychological state, playing its own role in the agent's motivational economy. Rather, that the agent has a relevant desire is a logical consequence of the fact that these considerations move him, a logical, but not a causal, condition for the efficacy of the beliefs.[3] It follows from the fact that these considerations move him that he has a relevant desire, but the desire is not a part of what moves him. We are left wondering just what this sort of desiring can be if

---

[3] I have been much helped in improving my understanding of Nagel's argument by the account given in Schueler (1995, ch. 1).

the fact that the agent so desires is logically entailed by facts that do not include it.

So much for an initial account of Nagel's position. In earlier work I objected to this position that it offers us an unacceptably hybrid theory of motivation (1993, ch. 2.1). This weakness stems from its admission that Humeanism is true much of the time. The position that Nagel takes himself to be attacking is one based, not on the distinction between two directions of fit, but on the distinction between two causal roles and on the claim that belief is totally inert. Belief normally needs desire to lead it because belief cannot cause anything on its own. As Nagel sees it, this claim is what lies at the heart of the Humean distinction between belief and desire; it is because of what belief is that it needs a certain sort of help from desire if it is to contribute to motivation. This being so, however, Nagel is not in a position to admit that the Humean story is true even some of the time. One cannot, that is, allow that belief generally needs an independent desire to cause it, since it is inert, and sometimes does not, since it is not inert. Nor can one say that some beliefs are inert and others are not, since the very same beliefs seem capable of playing now one role, and now the other. Nagel supposes that prudential beliefs are the ones that can on occasion play a non-Humean role. But it seems that there are no beliefs that are prudential simply in virtue of their content; even the belief that the cliff path is unstable is not intrinsically prudential. McDowell supposes that moral beliefs can play a non-Humean role; but he also supposes that in the non-virtuous person such beliefs play a Humean role. The Nagel–McDowell position therefore 'admits something that it cannot explain. By allowing that some motivation is Humean, even if other motivation is not, it allows that some beliefs need the help of desires if they are to motivate, and others do not, even though it can be the same beliefs both times. This is surely awkward, at best, and that was what the charge of hybridity was about.

There is some prospect, however, of a stronger criticism of Nagel's response to Humeanism. This is that it is irrelevant. This very strong charge will take a little while to build up.

Suppose we allow that motivated desires do not always stem from prior unmotivated ones. Now as far as the distinction between motivated and motivating desire goes, Nagel seems to have thought that the position he was attacking denies that belief is capable of causing desire, since it conceives of belief as totally inert. For otherwise a Humean could allow the motivated–motivating distinction, and appeal merely to the claim that for there to be an intentional action, there needs to be present in the agent a relevant belief–desire pairing. The Humean could say this without abandoning the standard distinction between two directions of fit. For even if the belief does cause the desire, the desire caused will still have the direction of fit that is standard for desire, and the belief will have that which is characteristic of belief. (Just as well, we may say; for the distinction between two directions of fit is the main formal account of the difference between belief and desire.) What the Humean would have to abandon is the conception of belief as inert. But we were not sure where that conception came from in the first place.

So, when Humeans claim that belief is incapable of motivating without the help of an independent desire, what do they mean by this? The answer to this question determines what is to count as a satisfactory refutation of their position. I think that people on both sides of this debate have been less clear than they might have been on this issue, leading both to some unnecessarily extravagant expressions of Humeanism and to some irrelevant 'refutations', including Nagel's.

I start with what I take to be a recognizable form of the Humean argument that moral judgements must be at least partly noncognitive. If we add to a purely cognitive state a moral judgement, is the result a complex state that is 'sufficient for action'? This phrase 'sufficient for action' is itself one of the difficulties. But the question that it is used to ask is not itself too obscure. It is whether, starting from a state that is purely cognitive, and adding to that state a moral judgement, it is conceivable that an intentional action should then occur *without further addition to, or other change in*, the psychological state of the agent. Humeans take it that the answer to this question is yes. And so, I suggest, do many others.

Humeans argue, however, that if the moral judgement is itself conceived as purely cognitive, the answer to our question would have had to be no. This is because they suppose that a purely cognitive state is incapable of motivating—is not and cannot be 'sufficient for action'—without the presence and help of an independent desire. And *ex hypothesi* the cognitive state we were concerned with in our question lacked such a helpful desire. So there could be no motivation, and so no action.

What do Humeans think about the possibility that a belief (or other purely cognitive state) should itself cause a desire in the agent? If such a thing is possible—and so far we have heard nothing to suggest it is impossible—it will be possible that a belief, finding itself incapable of causing an action in its present solitary state, should itself cause a suitable desire. By 'suitable' here, we mean a desire such that when it is combined with its parent belief, the resulting state is now 'sufficient for action'.

First, let us notice that Humeans should admit that this scenario is logically possible. It is surely a contingent matter what can cause what—a matter on which no Humean has dared to pronounce a priori. Beliefs, for Humeans, need not be devoid of causal consequences altogether. When it was said that belief is inert, it was not meant that beliefs have no consequences all their own; what was meant was that belief alone cannot motivate. A belief that causes a desire does not motivate it. Motivation is something to do with the generation of intentional action, action done for reasons. It is because of this that Humeans think that it requires both belief and desire. Desire is not action; or, if it were, Humeans *would* have a principled (a priori) reason for saying that belief alone cannot cause desire.

Suppose, then, that Humeans do admit that this scenario is possible. Is this admission itself fatal to their theory? I think not. But Nagel clearly supposes otherwise. What he offers is a prudential belief capable of making it the case that the agent has the required desire (a 'motivated' rather than a 'motivating' one). Since a motivated desire would not be a pre-existing desire, his target is clearly the sort of Humeanism that requires a *pre-existing* desire for motivation. But we should ask whether that sort of Humeanism is the only sort of Humeanism (let alone the best one).

What is required for Humeanism, then? If we cannot know a priori whether a belief can cause a desire, we can still know a priori that action and motivation require the presence of two independent states, a belief and a desire. We can also know why this is so; it is because of what it is to be a belief, and what it is to be a desire. It is because of what these two states are, and the differences between them (things knowable a priori), that we can know a priori that motivation and action require one of each. Knowing the difference between belief and desire is knowing the nature of a certain asymmetry between the contributions of the two states to motivation. Each requires the presence of the other; things are symmetrical in this weak sense. But the two states play quite different roles. We can try to capture these roles and the differences between them by saying that desire is a force and belief a channel for that force, or, preferably and much less metaphorically, by talking about two directions of fit. Whichever way we choose to do it, we are trying to capture the sense in which desire *leads* or *dominates* belief in motivation, i.e. when they are both present and motivating the same action. This is an asymmetrical relation, and it is one that is quite independent of the genealogy, the causal history, of the two states. For even if the belief causes a suitable desire, the relation between the belief and the desire in motivation will still be asymmetrical in that way.

To support this claim, we might point out that whatever sort of dominance Humeans want to talk about, it can perfectly well be found in a belief–desire pairing in which the desire is doing nothing to cause the belief, say where the belief and the desire are just co-present, neither causing the other. That neither is causing the other is no reason to deny the presence of Humean dominance, which derives from the very natures of belief and desire, not from how they happen to be related here. Why then should it be thought possible to argue that Humean dominance must be absent in any case where the belief causes the desire? There must surely be two forms of dominance. There is Humean dominance and causal dominance, and we can have the first even where neither belief nor desire causally dominates the other.

So an objection to Humeanism that depends solely on the distinction between motivated and unmotivated desire is therefore irrelevant. It leaves the core of its target untouched, concentrating only on the periphery. Nagel's real objection to Humeanism derives, not from the motivated–motivating distinction alone, but from that together with the further claim that the sort of desire that is necessary if there is to be an action may be only a logical consequence of the action, and not a required further causal factor. For if so, it is a genuinely cognitive state that is doing the motivating, and that the agent has the relevant desire is a mere consequence of that fact. The motivating state is now a truly non-Humean one, since it itself contains no desire at all.

I return to Nagel after characterizing what I take to be a position alternative to his.

Pure Cognitivism

Pure cognitivism, as I said in Chapter 1.5, supposes that a complete motivating state can consist of nothing but cognitive states. It allows that, where there is motivation, there will be desire. But it understands the desire as the state of being motivated rather than as some part of what motivates.

The argument for this purely cognitive picture of a motivating state is as follows. The explanation of motivation must be structurally similar to the explanation of action. For often the only thing necessary to take us from motivation to action is the absence of contrary motivation, or the fact that contrary motivations were 'weaker' than this motivation. The explanation of the action, then, will be the same as that of the motivation, together (perhaps) with the thought that competing motivations were either weaker or just absent. But the desire that is necessary if there is to be action is just a motivation; and we are understanding this as a state of being motivated—a motivatedness, as it were—rather than as what motivates. That state of being motivated will itself need an explanation, and this must now be given either in terms of the supposed nature of the thing desired—which, in psychologism's terms, would be to appeal to belief to explain desire—or in terms of a further desire. Either way, if motivation is to be eventually explained, it will be in terms of the (supposed) nature of that which motivates, which cannot itself be a desire and must be thought of as belief, if it is a psychological state at all.[4]

Some desires, of course, cannot be explained. But if they cannot be explained, then neither can the action that, in desiring as we do, we are motivated to perform. If we cannot say why we want to do it, the fact that we want to do it offers nothing by way of explanation for the action. It merely means that we

---

[4] Note that there is another way of understanding reference to 'the supposed nature of the thing desired' and 'the (supposed) nature of that which motivates', which will only become visible once we have moved away from psychologism at the end of Ch. 5. The point of the slightly complicated way I have put things in this paragraph is that the present attempt to dislodge desire, though expressed in psychologistic terms in favour of belief, can be expressed equally well in the 'realistic' terms that I will eventually come to adopt.

were, incomprehensibly, motivated to do this incomprehensible thing.

Here is another presentation of what I take to be the same argument, in greater detail. Suppose, first, that we are explaining an instance of A's ϕ-ing by appeal to the fact that A desired to ϕ, or to A's desire to ϕ. This is what one might call a 'buck-passing explanation'. *No* explanation has been given unless A's desire to ϕ can be explained. Further, if we explain an action by specifying what motivated it, as one naturally supposes, what motivated it cannot be the desire, for this only consists in the agent's being motivated; the action cannot be motivated by the agent's being motivated to do it. (Though it may be partly caused by this.) What motivates must therefore be that which underpins the desire. But the only thing that can underpin the desire and explain it appropriately is the nature of what is desired. All this does nothing to undermine the claim of desire to be a necessary part of whatever complex is capable of leading to action.

Suppose, second, that we are dealing with an instance of A's ϕ-ing which we are going to explain by appeal to the fact that A desired to ψ and that A supposed there to be some suitable relation between ϕ-ing and ψ-ing. This explanation is *not* a buck-passing explanation, even though it of course immediately raises a further explanatory question, namely why A desired to ψ. The desire to ϕ is a motivatedness which arises from the desire to ψ in virtue of means–end or other appropriate relations, as conceived by A. None the less, what motivates A to ϕ cannot be the desire to ψ. If that desire cannot be what motivates the action of ψ-ing, it cannot be what motivates the action of 'doing what promotes ψ-ing', namely ϕ-ing. The relation of motivation, that is, of motivating, if it cannot hold between ψ-ing and the desire to ψ, cannot hold between ψ-ing and doing what promotes ψ-ing. That desire must of course be a necessary part of whatever complex *led to A's* ϕ-ing, but it cannot be what *motivated* that action.

This argument rests on the idea that to desire is to be motivated. Why should we believe this? It is, of course, enormously plausible for a wide range of instances. Various people have produced lists of, as one might put it, types of desire. There are whims, biologically based desires (hunger, thirst, etc.), sudden urges and promptings, emotions (if these count as desires), desires that we have because we recognize good reason to want such a thing, and so on.

In all such cases, it seems plausible to equate the desire with being motivated. When one's desire is a Nagelian motivated desire, for instance, one is motivated not by the desire but by the reason that one perceives, understood as a belief. The desire does not occur until one is motivated, nor does it seem possible to have the desire without being motivated (though one can of course fight such a thing down or otherwise work to suppress it). In general, then, there seems no difficulty in identifying the desire with the motivatedness. Further, being motivated to act in certain ways is surely a state which has the direction of fit normally associated with desire, and it varies in strength as desire does.

Still, though I have not seen the point argued anywhere, potential counter-examples to the general identification of desiring with being motivated can be found. The obvious ones are desires concerning the past (as where I desire that my son should have got home safely last night) or concerning things in the future that I can do nothing about (as where, between the test and the result, I want it to turn out that I do not have the disease). There are also desires about the logical, and therefore uninfluenceable, as where I want this to be the right answer to the maths problem. Do such cases force me to withdraw my claim that to desire is to be motivated? This will depend on how we understand 'being motivated'. One possibility is this: that A is motivated to ϕ iff, were an opportunity of ϕ-ing to arise, A would seize it, in the absence of contrary motivation. There are problems with this as a definition, as one might expect. The first is that there is the standard danger of the conditional fallacy. It might be that A is now motivated to ϕ but would cease to be so motivated if an opportunity of ϕ-ing were to arise. The proposed definition of motivation also suffers from being unable to make any sense of the *strength* of motivation. But let us leave these difficulties to one side, supposing that in some way they can be met, and continue to take our initial definition as a stalking-horse. The counter-examples we considered shared a crucial feature, which was that no opportunity of acting to make what is desired actually take place could possibly arise. There is nothing one can do to change the past, or to make an incorrect mathematical proof be a correct one. We could cope with this by inserting the simple phrase *per impossibile* into the account of what it is to be motivated, thus:

A is motivated to ϕ iff, were an opportunity of ϕ-ing *per impossibile* to arise, *A* would seize it, in the absence of contrary motivation.

The question then is whether this insertion is a mere device. But I think that it is not. One of the unpleasant characteristics of these desires is just the sense that there is nothing that one can do about it. But this very sense of frustration (which has a clear phenomenology) reveals that there is here motivation that is indeed frustrated—motivation looking for an outlet and not finding it. And this is not at all the same as no motivation. It is like wanting very strongly to do something but having not the slightest idea how to set about it.

There are of course many things that one desires that one is not motivated to do, exactly, because they are not things that lie within one's capacities. I desire to die peacefully in my bed, but I am not, I think, motivated to do this, exactly. I am, however, motivated to do such things as may conduce to that desired result, which is all that the identification of desiring with being motivated requires.

Thomas Scanlon writes about what he calls 'desire in the directed attention sense' (1999: 43–5). He becomes interested in the prospect of buying a new computer, and finds himself looking in computer magazines, talking to people about the machines they have just bought, ringing up experts and asking about recent and likely future developments, and so on. Thoughts about his old machine and about the advantages he might get if he bought a better one intrude unwanted in contexts when they are not particularly apposite. He becomes prone to notice, and even to attach excessive significance to, comparatively minor defects in his present machine, and to such benefits as he will derive from a better one. And so on.

This is a recognizable syndrome, and we would certainly agree that such a person is desirous of a new machine. But it seems to me that the sort of behaviour that Scanlon describes is more a manifestation of desire than a sort of desire or a sense of 'desire'. I am left thinking that what is common to all desires (desirings) is that they are states of being motivated, and that Scanlon has characterized one way in which being motivated can express itself, often unfortunately for the person concerned.

I take it, then, that despite various difficulties, the identification of desiring with being motivated can be sustained.

Like desire, being motivated is a type of state that can feel like something to the person concerned. Desire can have a distinctive phenomenology. But it need not. Some motivatednesses, for instance cravings of certain types, definitely have a distinctive feel, while others, for instance my being motivated to have a look at a certain book when I am next in the library, do not. Just as, in the relevant thin sense of desire, there can be no action without desire, so, and for the very same reason, there can be no action without motivation. And so on. So I understand desire as a non-cognitive state, that of being motivated.

When we say that to desire is to be motivated, we are, of course, speaking of desire in the way to which philosophers have become accustomed, the way that makes it true rather than false that whatever we do we have at least some desire to do. It is this utterly general sense of 'desire' that makes it true that someone who very much does not want to be doing what he is doing none the less desires to do it. For it must be the case, if he is doing it intentionally, that he is motivated enough to do this despite his protestations of indifference, boredom, disinclination, and even disgust or abhorrence (even if we are wary of saying that he must be more motivated to do this than anything else, for reasons to do with weakness of will). Similarly, those who suffer from an obsessive-compulsive disorder, such as one that makes one wash one's hands 200 times a day (or many more, alas) or count up to fifty before writing each word, will deny vigorously that they want to do these things; they say that they *have* to do them.[5] Sometimes they just have to; sometimes something bad will occur if they don't. But either way, though they do not want to do these things, and may see nothing attractive about them, they are strongly motivated to do them, as we know since their lives are completely dominated by the perceived need to perform these rituals (Rapoport 1989).

I said earlier that Humeanism explains motivation by laying out the constitution of a motivating state, conceiving it as a combination of belief and desire. For the Humean, motivation is not something that happens next, as it were, once such a combination has been set up; to have such a combination is to be motivated to act

---

[5] Would it be right to say that they have a 'pro-attitude' towards doing these things? Somehow I doubt it, despite the frequence and casualness with which philosophers use this term. These agents do not seem to need a pro-attitude in order to be motivated.

in the appropriate way. What motivates one is that combination, and it motivates one to action. Pure cognitivism also attempts to 'explain motivation' by laying out the constitution of the relevant state, but it sees two such states, the state of being motivated and the state that motivates. The former is a desire and the latter is a belief or a combination of beliefs. If asked what motivates us to act, the answer cannot be 'a desire' unless this is intended in a purely trivial sense—that what motivates us to act is our being so motivated. The answer only looks non-trivial because of the case where we are motivated to do one action because we are motivated to do another, as where we are motivated to walk to the cupboard because we are motivated to have a drink (and the drinks are in the cupboard). But eventually we will get to a case where what motivates cannot be a desire. It cannot be that all the non-trivial answers eventually return us to a trivial one.

So pure cognitivism can agree with Humeanism on the following issues:

1. A complete motivating state consists entirely of psychological states of the agent.[6]
2. Belief and desire have distinct directions of fit.
3. A desire is an 'independent existence', perhaps with its own phenomenology. It is not a logical 'shadow' of the motivating beliefs, such as, for instance, the *fact* that the agent is motivated by those beliefs, but a distinct psychological state co-present with the beliefs when they motivate.
4. There can be no motivation without desire.

It disagrees with Humeanism about the composition of a motivating state, seeing such a state as consisting entirely of beliefs (or at least of states with the same direction of fit as that of belief).

So much by way of support for pure cognitivism. In this sort of area, however, what is needed to make a position attractive is not so much a direct argument in its favour, which I take myself now to have produced, but rather a detailed account of how it

---

[6] Pure cognitivism can even allow, with Humeanism, that a complete motivating state will normally consist of two distinct elements—so long as those elements are both cognitive. I suggested in Dancy (1993, ch. 1.5) that for motivation one normally needs beliefs both about how things stand at present and about how they will be if the action contemplated is successful; but I also mention possible exceptions to this rule (pp. 34–6).

manages to meet various requirements and circumvent various traps.

One such trap is the supposed existence of a very simple and completely knock-down argument for a broadly Humean theory of motivation, based on the distinction between two directions of fit. Michael Smith thinks that there is such a thing (1994: 116). But it still seems to me that the argument establishes far less than he supposes.[7] Here are its premisses:

(*a*) Having a motivating reason is, *inter alia*, having a goal.
(*b*) Having a goal is being in a state with which the world must fit.
(*c*) Being in a state with which the world must fit is desiring.

But what is the proper conclusion from these premisses? Smith wants:

(*d*) Desires are motivating reasons

but what he actually gets is:

(*d**) Having a motivating reason is, *inter alia*, desiring.

This is perfectly compatible with the claim that desires are not reasons of any sort, let alone motivating ones. Admittedly, to desire is to have a desire. But we would not be wise to move from

(1) To desire is to have a desire
(2) To desire is to have a motivating reason (*d**)

to

(3) A desire is a motivating reason.

To do so would be to rely on the hope that the 'having' relation is the same in (1) as in (2). It is not, as we can see if we rephrase (2) as 'To desire is to be motivated by some conception of how things are'.

In sum, the mere possibility of the view that having a desire is not what motivates but is rather a state of being motivated is sufficient to show that the argument from (*a*), (*b*), and (*c*) does not by itself establish (*d*).

A second worry concerns the way in which I argued that Nagel's rejection of Humeanism is irrelevant. I suggested that the

---

[7] See Dancy (1993, ch. 2).

cognitivist position should be that a purely cognitive state is 'sufficient for action', in the relevant sense; i.e. that, starting from a state
that is purely cognitive, it is conceivable that action should then
occur *without addition to, or other change in*, the psychological state
of the agent.

   In one way this is right, and the end of the matter. For if we once
showed that a purely cognitive state was sufficient for action in this
sense, we could show something similar about motivation. A purely
cognitive state can be sufficient for motivation, and is *thereby* sufficient for action, since action would then occur if there was no
stronger contrary motivation.

   The complications stem from the question whether desire plays
no role at all in either the story about motivation or the story about
action. Suppose that to be motivated *is* to desire. Then to be motivated is for a desire to occur, i.e. for a change to take place in one's
psychological state. Since there cannot be action without motivation, then even if we start from a state that is purely cognitive, it is
not conceivable that action should occur without addition to or
other change in the psychological state of the agent.

   But all that this shows is that I overstated the pure cognitivist
case. The crucial distinction here is between thinking of desire as
itself an essential part of a complete motivating state, and thinking
of it as identical with the state of being motivated—the state that
takes us from what motivates, at one end, to action at the other.
The point to stick to is that the motivating state is still fully cognitive. So if we are to make the required sense of our question 'Is a
purely cognitive state sufficient for action?', we have to read it as
'Is a purely cognitive state capable of being a complete motivating
state, i.e. to constitute the whole of that which motivates?' To this
question Humeans answer no, and, answering no, suppose that
moral judgement must at least contain a desire, on the grounds that
a purely cognitive state would become capable of being a complete
motivating state if we enriched it with a moral judgement. Pure cognitivism, by contrast, answers yes. For it holds that, starting from a
state that is purely cognitive, it is conceivable that *motivation*
should then occur *without addition to, or other change in*, that
psychological state of the agent to which the motivation (the motivatedness) is a response. What is more, even though there can
be neither motivation nor action without desire, the desire is not
what motivates either the agent or the action. The agent who

desires is motivated to action by (the prospect of getting) what he desires.

I now return to examine the differences between Nagel's position and my own. As we saw, he supposes that belief alone is capable of motivating, but that we properly speak of someone so motivated as wanting to do that which the belief gives him reason to do. He writes:

> *whatever* may be the motivation for someone's intentional pursuit of a goal, it becomes in virtue of his pursuit *ipso facto* appropriate to ascribe to him a desire for that goal. But if the desire is a motivated one, the explanation of it will be the same as the explanation of his pursuit, and it is by no means obvious that a desire must enter into this further explanation. (1970: 29)

So, of a person who acts in the light of a moral belief, we might *ascribe* to him the desire to do the right thing, but we should think of his so desiring only as a consequence of the fact that he is motivated by his belief that it is right, and not as the specification of a further independent element whose contribution is required if the belief is going to be able to motivate action.

Nagel thus defuses the Humean attack by allowing the need for a desire, but understanding this as entailed by the fact that the belief motivated the agent. He ties himself to no general position about motivated desires. Some may indeed be independent existences with the appropriate direction of fit; others may be merely consequentially ascribed.[8]

As I said earlier, this position escapes any charge of irrelevance. For it gives a non-Humean account of the structure of a complete motivating state as capable (at least) of consisting entirely of beliefs. It is, however, still liable to my other objection, that it is unacceptably hybrid. For, according to the 'pure ascription' theory, some motivating states are entirely cognitive, and others are not. Some consist of beliefs alone, and others consist of beliefs plus desires. What, then, is the difference between that sort of belief that

---

[8] In Dancy (1993, ch. 1) I took it that Nagel meant to think of all motivated desires as independently existing psychological states. I now recognize that I was wrong about this, mainly thanks to Schueler (1995). Bond (1983) supposes, by contrast, that for Nagel such desires amount really to no more than a way of talking; he makes great play with this in his criticisms of Nagel, in support of a standard Humean position about motivation. Bond was wrong too. Nagel just does not commit himself on the point.

is capable of motivation unaided and that which requires the presence of a quite different sort of state, a desire? We cannot suppose that there are two sorts of belief, one capable of functioning alone and the other not; for the very same belief may now be of one sort and now of the other. In one mood, as we might put it, any inability to do the job all on its own is made up by the addition of a further belief. In the other mood, no belief would be capable of filling the gap, and we have to insert a desire if we are to reach a complete motivating state. I do not really understand the suggestion that there are two sorts of gap to be filled, each accepting only one sort of filling and rejecting the other. This is the sort of thing that the charge of unacceptable hybridity is aimed at.

However we decide to move on these points, there is a clear difference between Nagel and the pure cognitivist. First, pure cognitivism gives exactly the same account of all desire. It does not see some desires as independently existing psychological states, contributing causally to motivation, and others as logical consequences of the fact that the agent is motivated. Second, pure cognitivism understands desire as required for motivation and action, not as an essential part of a complex cause, nor as a way of describing a situation that does not contain a desire as a component element, but as the state of being motivated which we cite motivating reasons to explain. This desire is an independently existing psychological state, with the appropriate direction of fit. It is neither a figure of speech nor part of what motivates.

Pure cognitivism has the advantage also that it takes Nagel's remarks about desire being a logically necessary condition to heart, and gives an explicit account of what this amounts to. That the agent has a relevant desire is entailed by the fact that he is motivated by a certain conception of how things are, since it just is the fact that he is motivated.

The final point in favour of pure cognitivism is that unlike Nagel's position it is not caught on the horns of a dilemma between being unacceptably hybrid and being irrelevant.

2. *Normativity and the Explanation of Action*

The previous section argued that if we are to understand motivation in terms of psychological states of the agent, we should think of those motivating states as entirely cognitive, contrary to the currently dominant view. The present section is a central hinge in this book, for in it I begin to ask whether this sort of approach to motivation is compatible with the account of good reasons developed in the two previous chapters. Here I do little more than set the scene for the argument that is to come in Chapter 5.

The explanation of an action succeeds to the extent that it enables us to see how the agent might have taken certain features of the action as good reasons to do it. Some explanations hardly achieve this at all. But the aim of doing so stands as what one might call a regulative ideal for the explanation of action. In this sense, to make a stab at explaining an action is to make at least the first moves towards a justification for it. We can of course justify an action without showing it to have been right. But there is an internal relation between justification and showing right, which is that the agent's motivating reasons are capable of justifying the action only if, were things as the agent supposed them to be, the action would have been right. So there is a sort of natural movement from attempting an explanation at one end to showing the action to have been right at the other.

In what sense, then, can we claim that the explanation of action is normative in style? In the weakest possible sense, we might say that we explain an action by seeking the best possible fit between (our interpretative accounts of) what the agent believes, what his purposes, aims, and desires are, what he means by what he says, and what he actually does. To the extent to which we can establish such a fit, we reveal the agent as approaching an ideal of rationality. Rationality here is conceived as a high degree of internal coherence of a complex sort. So there is normativity here. It is not entirely internal, for one of the matters that determines whether there is the sort of fit required between belief, desire, and action rests on the question whether, had the beliefs we attribute to the agent been true, they would have been good reason to do what we understand him as having done.

We move beyond this limited conception when we ask whether the agent's beliefs were ones that it was sensible to hold in the circumstances. And we move further beyond it if we ask whether things were as the agent believed, and whether what he wanted was really worth wanting. To the extent that we think it implausible that the agent thought this or wanted that, given

that what he thought was so crazy and what he wanted so blatantly unattractive, we move beyond questions of mere internal
coherence.

Donald Davidson seems to allow that these further matters all
bear on the question whether we have succeeded in explaining
what the agent did. He writes, 'In our need to make him make
sense, we will try for a theory that finds him consistent, a believer
of truths, and a lover of the good (all by our own lights, it goes
without saying)' (1980: 222). Perhaps we could add to this 'and a
doer of the sensible and the right'. Consistency here is to be understood as an internal criterion, and being a believer of truths and a
lover of the good is external.

John McDowell interprets the passage in which Davidson makes
this remark as intended to press the claims of an alternative form
of explanation, suited to the explanation of mental events (or of
events *qua* mental) but not to that of physical events. McDowell
writes:

To recognise the ideal status of the constitutive concept [of rationality] is
to appreciate that the concepts of the propositional attitudes have their
proper home in explanations of a certain sort: explanations in which things
are made intelligible by being revealed to be, or to approximate to being,
as they rationally ought to be. This is to be contrasted with a style of explanation in which one makes things intelligible by representing their coming
into being as a particular instance of how things generally tend to happen.
(1985: 389)

This seems right. The explanation of actions does succeed to the
extent that we are able to show that in doing this the agent ap-
proximated to being how he ought to be. For the internal and external conditions are normative conditions, expressed in terms of an
ideal by reference to which the individual is placed in the relevant
explanation. There is, as we might put it, an internal and an external norm in operation.

This gives us two 'levels' of normativity in standard Davidsonian
explanation of action. But there is a possible third level that goes
beyond these two, which emerges with the demand that the agent's
reason for acting must be capable of being a good one. This is the
level of normativity that interests me. What we have so far does not
address it, since we have only asked that things should, so far as
possible, be as the agent believes them to be. We have not yet asked

that the agent's reason for action, the motivating reason, should be capable of being a good reason.

Thomas Nagel considers the idea that the explanation of action must not be too far separated from the question whether there was good or sufficient reason to do what was done. He suggests that we do not simply 'drop out of the evaluative mode' when we ask why a person acted as he did. For if we did, our explanation would connect action with the agent's beliefs and desires, but would not have touched the question whether he had a *good* reason for acting. Nagel's view is that if this is all that can be said about why an agent acted, it would follow that we don't really act for reasons at all (1986: 142–3). Rather, we are caused to act by desires and beliefs, and the terminology of reasons can be used only in a diminished, non-normative sense to express the sort of explanation we are offering.

It is not clear quite how to understand these remarks of Nagel's. The idea must be that if explanation of action does not itself address at all the question whether the agent's reasons were good reasons, the sense in which it is capable of talking even of the agent's 'reasons' is in doubt. One way of understanding this is to think of the agent's own understanding of why he is doing what he is doing. The agent approaches things with the question 'Which option is the one that there is most reason to take?' If we relegate this question into the background when we come to give the explanation of the action, we subvert the purpose of explanation, which is to reveal the light in which the agent came to do what he did. That light is an evaluative light, and cannot be treated other than as such. If we do treat it in some other way, we stand back from the idea that, for the agent, the reasons why he is acting this way rather than that are good reasons. And if we do this, we undermine our right to speak of the agent acting for reasons in the first place.

Nagel's intention here is to attack claims that the explanation of action is to be achieved entirely by appeal to psychological states of the agent. As far as this goes, it does not matter whether those states are a combination of beliefs and desires, or just beliefs. So Nagel's remarks here call into question *all* the views discussed in this chapter, including, one would have thought, those of his earlier book. In the next chapter I consider whether he is right to be so critical of belief–desire explanation of action, and of psychologism in general.

5

Acting for a Good Reason

1. *Psychologism: The Three-Part Story and the Normative Story*

Psychologism is a view about motivation; it is the claim that the reasons for which we act are psychological states of ourselves. Nagel's claim, by contrast, was that if we explain actions by appeal to the beliefs and desires of the agent, we will have to abandon any suggestion that agents act for reasons. We explain an intentional action by specifying the reasons that motivated the agent. So Nagel is claiming that if we adopt psychologism, we might as well give up talking about acting for a reason altogether. The present chapter is intended to provide support for this view of Nagel's. In writing it, I will be assuming that the form of psychologism to be attacked is the best form, namely pure cognitivism. This has the great advantage that we do not have to introduce complicating considerations about desires. The only psychological states relevant are beliefs, and we can discuss the matter entirely in terms of the relation between the belief (the believing, that is) and the thing believed.

In this chapter, and to some extent in the next, I will operate with a terminology which I have been largely avoiding up to now. This is the terminology of motivating reasons and normative reasons. I have tried in earlier chapters to speak rather of the reasons that motivate us, as contrasted with good reasons—the latter being reasons for being motivated or for doing the action. My purpose was to avoid even appearing to commit myself to the view that there are two *sorts* of reason: the motivating sort and the normative or good sort. Instead I stressed the idea that we use one and the same notion of a reason in answer to two distinct sorts of question, the question why someone acted and the question whether there was good reason so to act. All the issues I have discussed could have been discussed in terms of the contrast between motivating reasons and normative reasons, had it not been for the unwanted implication carried by that terminology. (Indeed, this is how I did things in earlier drafts of this book.) Now, however, I want to relax my ban on that terminology for a while. This is because the positions that I am here working to reject are best formulated in its terms. Those positions do hold that though we speak of motivating *reasons* and normative or good *reasons*, we are genuinely dealing with two distinct *sorts* of reason, in a way that raises the question whether the word 'reason' is not awkwardly ambiguous. I am going to allow this way of speaking in the course of an attempt to argue that it is incoherent.

So—are any motivating reasons psychological states of the agent? As I said before in Chapter 1 (p. 15) above, the sorts of reason we actually give, in explaining either our own actions or those of others, seem to be characterized sometimes in terms of a psychological state of the agent, and sometimes not. I might say that we are sending our child to this school because we believe it will suit her better; and I might say that I am taking my car down to the garage because it is time for it to be serviced. Admittedly, in the second sort of case, I must believe that it is time for a service if I am to act in the light of that fact. But still it seems to be not so much my believing this as what I believe that is being offered as my reason for doing what I propose to do. So, we may say, some reason-giving offers a belief of the agent as a reason, and some offers what is believed by the agent instead; and there is a world of difference between these. If our motivating reasons are all 'what is believed', no reasons are psychological states of the agent. If those reasons are all psychological states of the agent, none are properly, fully specifiable in the form '*A* acted because *p*'. The proper, philosophically revealing form will be '*A* acted because *A* believed that *p*'; and we will understand this sort of explanation as specifying a psychological state of the agent as *explanans*.

Psychologism has a large and enthusiastic following. But any complete theory of practical reasons has to deal not only with motivating reasons but also with normative reasons. With that in mind, three possibilities are available for us. We can understand both normative and motivating reasons as psychological states of the agent. We can understand all reasons as what the agents believe, rather than as their believings of those things. Or, finally, we can hold that motivating reasons are psychological states of the agent, while normative reasons are what agents (we hope) believe.

Of these three possibilities, I think that the first is clearly implausible. It is implausible because it is so extreme. It is not the view that all normative reasons are *grounded in* psychological states of the agent. The desire-based view, which holds that all practical reasons derive their normative status from a relation to some desire of the agent, is of that sort; and it is worth arguing against. But the view we are currently considering is that all normative reasons *are* psychological states of the agent. This would rule out any such reasons as that she asked me to do it, that this is an opportunity I have long been waiting for, and that I will be too busy to have time to do it next week. There would have to be an amazingly strong argument to persuade us that considerations like these are altogether of the wrong sort to count as reasons in favour of an action. The only argument that I can see in the offing is that all motivating reasons are psychological states of the agent, and that normative reasons must be a subset of motivating reasons. Whatever the merits of such an argument (and I confess that it would seem to me to vindicate Nagel's view that psychologism should cause us to abandon the very idea of acting for a reason), it returns us to the question whether motivating reasons are or are not psychological states.

What I want to examine, then, are the respective merits of the second and the third possibilities. I am interested in promoting the second alternative, under which no reasons at all, neither motivating nor normative, are psychological states of the agent. But this requires me to argue against a position that appears well entrenched. It is worth taking a moment to build up an initial version of this third theory, as follows.

We have already noticed that when we speak of reasons for action, the little word 'for' cloaks an ambiguity, or at least a distinction. There are reasons in favour of acting, and reasons why we acted. Favouring is one thing; it is a normative relation, and the reasons that favour actions can include such things as normative states of the world, for certainly they are unlikely to be psychological states of the agent. The reasons why we act, however, are not themselves things that favour actions; they are things that explain them. These are all psychological states of the agent—

believings, if pure cognitivism is the truth; pairs of believings and desirings, if it is not. Now there is a constraint on any theory about the relation between normative and motivating reasons. This is that the theory show that and how any normative reason is capable of contributing to the explanation of an action that is done for that reason. Call this the 'explanatory constraint'. There is a way in which it is easy to meet that constraint. The believings that explain the action can themselves be explained, of course, and on occasions at least we do so by appeal to their truth. He believed that there was a rhinoceros before him because there was one there; she believed that he needed her help because he did. So the reasons that favour an action can explain the reasons that explain the action. So though normative reasons do not explain actions directly, they explain them indirectly. The explanatory constraint is met by appeal to the transitivity of explanation. We emerge with a three-part story in which everything has its place, and nothing is missed out. The story is: normative reason → motivating reason → action. The arrows in this story indicate relations of explanation, though of course there is more to the matter than those explanatory relations alone.

Opposed to this three-part story is one which denies the existence of motivating states as reasons of any sort, and tries to make do with normative reasons. These normative reasons are also able to play the role of motivating reasons; that is, in ordinary English, the reason why we should act is to be (at least able to be) the reason why we do act. What is believed is what motivates us as well as what makes it the case that what we did was the right thing to have done. The believing, which of course occurs (though even this will be questioned), does not play the role of motivating reason; some other role must be found for it. Motivating reasons are what is believed; and some of the things believed are normative reasons as well.

Let us call this alternative story the 'normative story', because it takes its start from normative reasons. It is obviously going to be hard to develop, let alone sustain. In order to gain it some credibility, as it were, I am now going to run through a list of potential objections to the three-part story. For if the three-part story collapses under attack, the prospects for the normative story are obviously much better.

2. *Against the Three-Part Story*

I start by considering a standard argument *for* the claim that motivating reasons are psychological states of the agent, specifically believings, which runs as follows:

The statement

    (1) A's reason for ϕ-ing was that p

can only be true if

    (2) A believed that p.

Therefore

    (3) A's reason for ϕ-ing was that A believed that p.

This argument is of course rather peculiar and not obviously valid. But I want to say two further things about it. The first is that it is not an argument for psychologism. Its conclusion is not that A's reason for ϕ-ing was his believing that p, but that his reason was that he believed that p. That is to say, the motivating reason it 'discovers' is not itself a psychological state of the agent but the 'fact' that the agent was in such a state. That A believed that p is not itself a psychological state of A's. If it were, A could be in it; but the sense in which A is *in* the fact that A believed that p is surely not the sense in which A is *in* a psychological state.

We could of course rewrite the argument with, as its conclusion, not (3) but the genuinely psychologistic

    (3*) A's reason for ϕ-ing was A's believing that p.

The point I am trying to make, however, is directed at those who have become psycholog*ists*, in my sense, by arguing for (3) and then misunderstanding their own conclusion as the psychologistic (3*)— a train of thought which I take to be fairly common.

Second, the argument as I have given it above says nothing about how it is to be interpreted. In particular, it does not say whether its 'conclusion' is to be understood as replacing its first premiss, or as related to that premiss in some other way. I don't want to suggest that there would be any incoherence in an argument whose conclusion is inconsistent with one of its premisses. We are all used to such things. The point is rather that, for all the argument tells us, it may be that the conclusion is intended as a sort of philosophical explication of, rather than a replacement for, the premiss. In general, as will emerge, I have no quarrel with the idea that (1) and (3) are somehow more or less equivalent, i.e. that (3) is a restatement of (1). It is true that we move without strain from the simple form of action-explanation (1) to the psychologized form (3) and back again. We should accept this and cater for it in our overall account of the explanation of action. Problems only arise when it is supposed that (1) is an incomplete specification of a reason that is only fully characterized by (3)—something on which the argument given above is officially silent. In my view, if there is a difference between (1) and (3), it speaks entirely in favour of (1) as the normal form in which to give a reason. But I have still to argue for this view. (The argument comes in Chapter 6.1.)

It is one thing, however, to undermine supposed arguments for a position, and another to show the position itself to be false. So I now make three direct objections to the three-part story. The first is one that I have already offered in print.[1] This objection amounts to the introduction of a further constraint, which we can call the normative constraint, in addition to the explanatory constraint that we have already seen. This requires that a motivating reason, that in the light of which one acts, must be the sort of thing that is capable of being among the reasons in favour of so acting; it must, in this sense, be possible to act for a good reason. The explanatory constraint held that all normative reasons should be the right sort of thing to contribute to motivation, since that is what they must be if they are to be capable of contributing to the explanation of action in the right sort of way. The normative constraint goes in the other direction, claiming that motivating reasons should be the right sort of thing to be normative reasons.

The three-part story fails the normative constraint in a very blatant way, for it renders us more or less incapable of doing an action for any of the reasons that make it right. It makes it impossible, that is, for the reasons why we act to be *among* the reasons in favour of acting. If I am trying to decide what to do, I decide which action is right, noticing (we hope) the reasons that make it right; and then I act in the light of those reasons. They are the reasons why I do what I do (my motivating reasons). According to the three-part story, this is impossible. For the three-part story announces that motivating reasons are psychological states and

[1] See Dancy (1995a, 1996, 2000a).

that normative reasons are quite different, including even such things as normative facts about the world. The three-part story has set itself up in such a way that it is bound to breach the normative constraint; which is to say that it has introduced far too great a gap between the explanatory and the normative. And this makes the three-part story paradoxical at its core.

It is not just that, by thinking of motivating reasons as psychological states of the agent, the three-part story breaches the normative constraint. I want to agree with psychologism that we should not be looking among psychological states of the agent for the normative reasons that favour the action. The psychologists are right about this. For no—or only very few—psychological states of the agent are normative reasons; it is not normally psychological states of the agent that make his action the right one to do. In a way I expect this point to be obvious. What makes my action wrong is that she badly needed help and I just walked away from her. What makes overtaking on the wrong side of a bend not a very sensible thing to do is that there may well be something coming the other way. Once one has started in this vein one can go on for ever. Psychologism must be right to think of normative reasons as facts, as states of affairs, or as features of the situation, and must be wrong, therefore, to think of motivating reasons as psychological states of the agent.

What confuses the issue is that it is possible to think that the agent's mental states do make a difference to the question whether he acted rightly. And so they do, in a way; for that he believed she would welcome his advances surely makes him (or his action) less reprehensible than he (or it) would have been if he had believed the opposite, especially if his belief was reasonable. But, first, that belief, even if reasonable, need not make the action right. As we saw in Chapter 3, his believing this can serve as some defence or excuse for his doing what he did, without making that action right. The normative relevance of the belief lies primarily at the evaluative level, rather than at the deontic level where reasons lie. And, second, there remains the awkward difference between the suggestion that it is his belief, conceived as a mental state that he is in, that is the reason and the suggestion that it is that he so believes that is the reason. For that he so believes is not a mental state that he is in, but a state of affairs; just as his nervousness is a mental state that he is in, but that he is nervous is a state of affairs rather than a mental state. At the moment we are only discussing the less plausible view that the normative reason is a mental state of the agent.

In these matters, I am mindful of the results reached in Chapters 2 and 3, when, having tried to understand the requirements of rationality and morality as somehow relative to the beliefs (and the desires) of the agent, we were forced first to allow that some requirements cannot be so expressed, and second to accept that all requirements (of either sort) are objective rather than relative in the way suggested. If this result was correct, it cannot be the case that all normative reasons consist in psychological states of the agent.

I have been trying to show that the three-part story is committed to the paradoxical claim that it is impossible to do an action for the reason that makes it right. As I put it earlier, the reasons why we act can never be among the reasons in favour of acting, if the three-part story is true. This paradox is even more marked in the theory of theoretical reasons (reasons for belief) than in the theory of practical reasons. We could tell a three-part story there too: the reasons why we believe things are always other beliefs of ours— other believings, that is—and the reason why we are right to adopt those beliefs is the evidence available, or something like that. The evidence available explains our believings, and those believings explain our adopting this new belief. This three-part story has the same paradoxical consequence, that none of the reasons why we believe something is ever a reason in favour of believing it. The reasons why we believe something will always be other psychological states of ours, never anything like the evidence available to us.

In my now fairly wide experience, the normal response of those attracted to the three-part story is to say, when accused of paradox in this sort of way, that the matter is wildly exaggerated. The normative reason, they say, can perfectly well be thought of as a motivating reason in any case where its being the case that p makes right an action that is done because of the belief that p. For if A explains B and B explains C, A is part of the explanation of C; and motivating reasons include anything that contributes to the explanation of the action. But this seems to me not so much to defend the story as to abandon it. The core of the three-part story is the claim that normative reasons cannot be motivating ones, a claim that rests on psychologism about motivating reasons and a (correct) sense that normative reasons are in general nothing like psychological states of the agent. The sorts of thing that are normative reasons are things like the pain the other is suffering, the wrong I will be doing her if I persist, and other features of the world that call for certain responses from us. These normatively significant states of affairs are metaphysically different beasts from psychological states of the agent. Having insisted on this difference, the three-part story cannot then go on to ignore it, and to say in spite of it that we can perfectly well speak of those normative states of affairs as motivating reasons, even though their official view (indeed, the core of their position) is that only psychological states of the agent can play that role. This would be far too much like trying to have one's cake and eat it.

Despite this, there may be some truth in the complaint that my attack on the three-part story involves some exaggeration, and for this reason I am not sure quite how much to rest on it. In some moods it seems to me to be annihilating; in others it seems more like nitpicking. The problem is that the attack rests an enormous amount on the possibility that motivating and normative reasons should be capable of being identical. The appeal is to such expressions as 'The reason for which he did it was a very good one' or, more philosophically, 'It must be possible for the reasons in the light of which one acts to be *among* the reasons in favour of doing what one does'. If someone said that these expressions do not need to be taken *au pied de la lettre*, it is not obvious what I have to say in reply.

So I turn now to my second criticism of the three-part story. This is just a slightly different and simpler way of making the point that the separation it introduces between the explanatory and the normative is too sharp. We normally try to explain an action by showing that it was done for good reason, or at least for what might reasonably have been thought to be good reason at the time. But psychological states of the agent are the wrong sorts of thing to be good reasons. A believing cannot be a good reason for acting, because a good reason for acting is a reason that favours acting, and such things, according to the three-part story, are states of the world, not psychological states of the agent. What is more, the three-part story is right about this. What makes my action right in the circumstances is very rarely any psychological state of mine, as we have seen.

Here we see again why it is important to speak of normative reasons rather than, as is common, of justifying reasons. For one's having reasonably believed that p is often offered as a justification of one's action in cases where it turns out that it was not the case that p. And it may indeed succeed in *justifying* one's having acted as one did, that is, in defending one against certain charges, without this meaning that it is able to play the role of a normative reason. As I have suggested several times now, my having (reasonably) believed that p is only able to justify my action if, had it been the case that p, I would have been acting rightly, doing the right thing. The normative reason here would be that p, not my having believed that p. My believing that p is not a reason for action in either sense (or of either sort); it is at best a justification for my having acted as I did.

Perhaps this criticism of the three-part story is not in the end distinct from the first; on any account it is not much more than a generalization of it. It amounts to little more than the claims that a reason for acting (a motivating reason) must be the right sort of thing to be a good reason, and that a good reason is a normative reason. Again, the three-part story meets the explanatory constraint but fails the normative constraint. The important point for present purposes is that this second criticism seems less vulnerable to the charge that it involves a certain exaggeration. There is not so much hanging on the demand for potential *identity* between motivating and normative reasons—at least nothing is hanging on that alone. The need for the potential identity is itself supported by the need for motivating reasons to be of the right sort to be good reasons. If only normative reasons can be good reasons, and if reasons (of whatever sort) must be able to be good or less good, then only the sorts of thing that are normative reasons can be motivating reasons.

The crucial point here is that believing that p is never (or hardly ever) a good reason for ϕ-ing. It is what is believed, that p, that is the good reason for ϕ-ing, if there is one.

Finally, I want to stress one feature of this argument. This is the constant stress on the phrase 'right *sort of* thing'. A motivating reason must, I claimed, be the right sort of thing to be a normative reason. This is really a metaphysical point. Some motivating reasons cannot be good reasons. Perhaps the downfall of others cannot be a good reason for satisfaction. Perhaps, as some hold, the rightness of an action cannot be among the reasons for doing it. But these features are still, metaphysically speaking, the right sort of thing to be a good reason. They are ruled out, if they are indeed ruled out, not by being the wrong sort of thing, but by being wrong ones of the right sort. (There is more on this in Chapter 7.)

These, then, are my first two arguments against the three-part story. My third argument is much more controversial. Arthur Collins has argued that the three-part story makes possible something that is in fact impossible, namely for the agent to explain his action in a way that makes no commitment to the truth of the beliefs that he cites in that explanation (Collins 1997).

The aim of the explanation of action is to give, so far as possible, the agent's own perspective on things, so as to reveal the light in which the action was done. The subject-matter of the explanation is not the agent's perspective; that perspective is the one from which the explanation is made, but that it is so made is not itself part of the explanation. The subject-matter of the explanation is 'the objective circumstances' (as Collins puts it) as apprehended by the agent, not the agent's apprehension of those circumstances.

Consider now an explanation as offered by the agent; he says 'I am doing this because I believe that p'. Collins calls this sort of explanation, with which as such he has no quarrel, a 'psychologizing restatement' of the briefer explanation that runs 'I am doing this because p'. The agent might move, or be forced to move, to the psychologized explanation because he recognizes that he might well be mistaken in his belief that p. He might even go so far as to say 'I am doing this because, though I may be wrong about this, I believe that p'. What then is the relation between these variously expressed explanations? The simple explanation 'I am doing this because p' clearly expresses the speaker's endorsement of or commitment to the claim that p. No explanation that obliterated that endorsement would be the correct explanation of the action, since it would fail to give the agent's perspective on things, and hence fail to capture the light in which the action was done. The psychologizing restatement offered by the agent must therefore be understood as retaining that endorsement (as discussion of Moore's Paradox encourages us to suppose), and its effectiveness as an explanation depends on this fact. Further, in accepting the psychologized restatement of his reason, the agent is not supposing that the subject-matter of the explanation has thereby been

changed from the (supposed) objective circumstances to the subjective nature of the agent. So we have it that the psychologizing
restatement of the original explanation must satisfy the following
conditions:

1. It does not introduce a new subject-matter;
2. It does not somehow delete the agent's endorsement.

But these two conditions are not met by the way in which the three-
part story understands what is going on in what it takes to be the
move from the original briefer explanation to the psychologizing restatement. The two stages in the three-part story may be
understood as two parts of a complex explanation. First there is
the 'proximal' explanation of the action, given by specifying the
psychological state of the agent. Then there is the 'distal' explanation of the action, given by specifying what is responsible for the
agent getting into that state. The distal explanation of the action is
the proximal explanation of the psychological state. So the three-
part story takes there to be considerable differences between the
subject-matters of the two explanations. We can easily imagine
saying of another that he acted because he believed that p, though
it was not in fact the case that p, and his believing that p has to be
explained in another way. Here we avoid committing ourselves to
the things that the agent was committed to, things his commitment
to which explains his action. We take ourselves, supposedly, to be
giving a proximal explanation of the action in a way that avoids any
commitment on the appropriate distal explanation. The point that
Collins makes here is that this form of uncommitted explanation
is never available to the agent, for reasons to do with Moore's
Paradox. The agent himself cannot explain his action by appeal to
a belief he currently has without committing himself to the truth
of that belief. He cannot say 'I am doing it because I believe that
p' in any way that stands back from his commitment to its being
the case that p. So the distinction between proximal and distal
explanation, which is a central element in the three-part story's
understanding of what is going on, distorts the nature of the
explanation of action.

This argument of Collins's is extraordinarily difficult to grasp
clearly. Here is another attempt to make his point, more briefly. The
agent takes 'I am doing it because p' and 'I am doing it because I
believe that p' as equivalent explanations. The second explanation

does not have a new and quite different subject-matter, the psychology of the agent rather than its being the case that p. And it does not in this or any other way cancel the agent's endorsement of or commitment to its being that case that p. It is not, for the agent, as if the second explanation does something very different from the first. It is not, in particular, as if the second explanation mentions an intermediate stage in the explanatory flow, not alluded to by the first explanation. Nor does the second explanation enjoy other advantages, such as that by a change of subject-matter it specifies something that the agent is less likely to have been wrong about. *It is really the same explanation both times.* Any difference between them affects not so much the nature of the explanation offered as the form in which it is presented. So much from the agent's point of view. Now since our third-person explanation of the action should be, so far as possible, the agent's explanation, we too should not take the psychologized restatement of the original explanation to be doing a different job from that done by the unpsychologized reasons-statement. In particular, we should not see it as specifying a proximal as opposed to a distal stage in the explanatory flow. We have to understand the psychologizing restatement in some other way—in a way that somehow respects the fact that for the agent the psychologized and the non-psychologized explanations are effectively identical.

We might reply that the distal–proximal distinction is forced upon us by the existence of cases where things are not as the agent conceives them to be. Where the agent says 'I am doing it because p' and it is not the case that p, we cannot offer for ourselves the explanation that he offers. His explanation is mistaken. The truth of the matter is that he is doing it because he believes that p. Since it is not the case that p, that p cannot explain anything; the explanation must lie in the fact that he believes, mistakenly, that p.

I shall return to this matter in Chapter 6 and again in Chapter 7, but it is worth quoting here Collins's reply to this objection. 'It is his reason, and in case he is wrong he acts because he makes this error. No claim asserting some other matter about which he is not in error [e.g. that he believes that p] can be substituted in rendering his reason for acting' (1997: 123). One might paraphrase this as follows. If he is wrong, still he acts because of the way in which he takes things to be, a matter on which he is mistaken. It would distort things to suppose that his reason for acting was something else about which he is not wrong, such as that he so takes things to be. Even more simply: either the reason for which he acts is something that is the case, or it is something that is not the case. In the second instance, we do not need to locate something else that is the case to be the reason for which he acts.

This argument of Collins's is much more radical than the two I offered before. He is disputing the standard understanding of the belief-attributions that are supposed to specify motivating reasons. In my first two criticisms on the three-part story I saw no reason to deny that belief-attributions characterize psychological states of the agent, while Collins eventually denies that beliefs are psychological states at all. They are stances but not states. For if they were states, the statement 'I believe that *p*' would have to be thought of as alluding to the existence in me of such a state, and so have quite a different subject-matter from that of the simple statement that *p*. In slightly more detail, Collins's argument here is as follows:

(1) If there are inner states of belief that *p*, then the existence of such a state does not require it to be true that *p*. This is guaranteed by the fact that some beliefs are false.

(2) Therefore, to say that the inner state of belief that *p* is present in *A* is not to say it is true that *p*. It does not express any stand on whether it is the case that *p* or not, something that is a different and independent matter of fact.

(3) (2) obtains even if it is *A* himself who says (reports) the presence of the inner state.

(4) If believing that *p* is an inner state, *A* can state that he believes that *p* (the inner state is present) without expressing a stand on whether it is the case that *p*.

(5) Since *A* cannot do this, believing that *p* is not an inner state.[2]

For this reason it does not seem that Collins's views can be seen as an expansion of Nagel's point, unless that point has ramifications that Nagel was not aware of.

A question then arises whether the attack on the three-part story can stop short of this more radical claim. And this question becomes more pressing when we recognize that there are powerful reasons to hold that beliefs are not psychological states at all, not especially for reasons to do with Moore's Paradox, but more

---

[2] Thanks to Arthur Collins for this perspicuous representation of the main argument of Collins (1987).

for reasons to do with the duration of belief and other features in which belief differs from standard or paradigm examples of psychological states.[3] If this more radical position were sound, the whole of the three-part story would be blown apart. For the three-part story to work, motivating reasons must be states of the agent, caused in certain ways and causing intentional actions. If there are no such things in the first place, the story collapses.

3. *Explanation by Appeal to Content*

One aspect of the three-part story that I did not criticize concerns the way in which it sought to meet the explanatory constraint. It did this by announcing that the belief which explains the action, the belief that *p*, is itself to be explained by its being the case that *p*. That *p*, therefore, can be understood as a part of the explanation of the action, even though properly it is only contributing to the explanation at one remove, distally, as it were.

Against this we might say that it is actually quite rare for a belief to be explicable by appeal to things being as they are believed to be. To be sure, there are cases in which this is appropriate. But in many, perhaps most, it is not. That it is about to rain may explain why everyone is coming in. Is their belief that it is about to rain to be explained by its being about to rain? Or is it rather the blackness of the clouds and the sudden drop in temperature? These are not themselves to be explained by its being about to rain. The clouds are not black *because* it will shortly rain. The same is very often true in the case that really concerns me, the explanation of moral action. Suppose I act as I do because I believe it to be my duty. Is it at all convincing to suggest that my belief may itself be explained by appeal to the fact that it is my duty? More convincing explanations seem to be available, such as my moral upbringing. That things are as I take them to be does not seem likely to enter into *these* explanations.

We do not have to agree with all these points to wonder whether the three-part story was really the strongest version of psychologism. The appeal to the transitivity of explanation was nice; but perhaps it turns out to be more of a liability than a strength—a lia-

[3] See Hacker (1992); Hunter (1980); Malcolm (1991).

bility to be added to the weaknesses already exposed. There may be other ways of constructing a psychologistic account of motivating reasons. The one that suggests itself most forcibly involves the notion of content. The idea here is that the motivating reason is the psychological state of the agent, the believings he is currently engaged in, and the normative reason is the content of those believings. The content of a belief is here being understood as (and only as) *what is believed*. Since I have tied myself to the view that normative reasons are what is believed, e.g. that she needs my help, I should be happy about this. But it is further suggested that what is believed can contribute to the explanation of the action, since the believing comes *with* a content, and needs to do so if it is to explain anything. So it is psychological state *plus* content that together constitute the motivating reason, and the content alone that constitutes the normative reason, if there is one.

It is worth pressing the question whether the content-based approach does really meet our two constraints: the explanatory constraint that a normative reason must be at least capable of contributing to the explanation of an action that is done in the light of that reason, and the normative constraint that motivating reasons must be at least capable of being good reasons. One might say, I suppose, that the appeal to content does succeed in meeting both constraints, more or less. The normative reason contributes to the explanation of action by being a vital part of the motivating reason. The motivating reason is capable of being a good reason in the sense that its content is so capable. Still, if I am to stick to my two constraints, the fact remains that we are here trying to conceive of motivating reasons as psychological states of the agent, with real reasons, as one might put it, as content. The sort of motivating reason we are offering is itself incapable of being a good reason (except in certain very special cases). What is more, it will not be the sort of reason we specify when we lay out the light in which he acted, for that light will not consist in certain psychological states of his.

Psychologism, as a theory of motivating reasons, holds that only states can motivate. Contents, however conceived, cannot do it. Equally, a content can be a good reason for action but a psychological state cannot (at least not normally). We do not achieve theoretical equilibrium by amalgamating these two remarks, eliding the bits that we do not want, and hoping that they will thereby be able to make up a conception of how we can do an action for the reason that makes it right. The combination of state and content is torn apart in its attempt to be (able to be) both normative and motivating. If the problem is how to get one thing that can do both, this form of conceptual cookery is not the solution.

None the less, I know that many will think that, in these remarks, I am taking my two constraints, especially the normative one, far more literally than can be justified. We agree that literally speaking the motivating reason is not itself capable of being a normative reason. But it is close enough to what *is* capable of being a normative reason, we may say, for all practical (and indeed theoretical) purposes. And indeed, despite these initial misgivings, I do find the content-based approach much more persuasive than the three-part story. But I am going to suggest that the philosophy of mind that is needed to make it work is going to have to be pretty outlandish. In glossing the content of a belief simply as 'what is believed', I was trying to make it appear that the content-based form of psychologism was not committed to any particular philosophical account of what content is to be. But the fact remains that if this content-based version is to be successful, it must give some account of content that shows how the contents of our beliefs are capable of doing what is here required of them. This really means that we must abandon the standard understanding of the contents of beliefs as propositions believed. For what we are now counting as contents must be capable of playing two roles:

1. They must be able to be good reasons for action (and for belief);
2. They must be the sort of thing that can be believed and be not believed, and can be believed both truly and falsely.

I want to suggest that propositions, even true ones, are incapable of playing at least the first of these roles. Propositions are incapable of being good reasons for action. So if they do indeed count as what we believe, the content-based strategy in its present form is broken-backed.

My first and simplest point here is that intuitively it seems to be not so much propositions as states of affairs that are our good reasons. It is her being ill that gives me reason to send for the doctor, and this is a state of affairs, something that is part of the world, not a proposition. Those who announce that all good reasons are propositions (e.g. Scanlon 1999: 57) seem thereby to lose contact with the realities that call for action from us.

In case this point should not be persuasive, I support it by considering in more detail what sort of thing a proposition is supposed to be, and asking whether anything like that could be a good reason. There are many different understandings of what propositions are, but I will just look at the two leading accounts, or perhaps groups of accounts. The first of these understands a proposition as what is expressed by an assertoric or indicative sentence, and what such a sentence expresses is itself understood in terms of a distinction between two sets of possible worlds, those in which the sentence is true and those in which it is false. We can define the proposition expressed by the sentence 'Canberra is hot in February' as the class of worlds in which that sentence is true.[4] The second understanding of propositions sees them as abstract objects that have the sort of structure that an assertoric sentence has. So the proposition that Canberra is hot in February is a structured object with constituents that correspond to the elements of the sentence 'Canberra is hot in February'. It is an abstract object that consists of Canberra, of being hot, and of certain times of the year, perhaps, and of the relation between these things that would make it the case that Canberra is hot in February, all placed in a suitable structure analogous to that of the relevant sentence. Now the question is whether on either account (remembering that both accounts are hotly disputed) propositions are the right sort of thing to be good reasons for action. It seems just obvious that they are not. For a class of worlds is hardly the right sort of thing to make an action sensible or right. And an abstract object with a structure that mirrors that of a sentence seems to be no better off. On either understanding, propositions are, as we might say, too thin or insubstantial to be able to make an action wrong. They are the wrong sort of beast. Reasons for action are things like his self-satisfaction, her distress, yesterday's bad weather, and the current state of the dollar. They cannot be abstract objects of the sort that propositions are generally supposed to be.

Of course we do, or at least can, say such things as 'That she is in distress is what made his action callous, and that she is in

---

[4] Stalnaker suggests that propositions are functions from possible worlds to truth values (1984: 2); I would say the same about propositions understood in this way as I say about propositions as sets of worlds in the main text.

distress is a proposition'. But this should not persuade us that the very thing that made his action callous is a proposition. We also say things like 'That the cliff was unstable was a consequence of the heavy rain, and that the cliff was unstable is a proposition', but we would surely be unwise to conclude from this that a proposition was a consequence of the heavy rain. It may be that by her action she ensured that she would not run out of petrol before reaching London; but what she ensured was not a proposition. In general, though we use that-clauses to specify propositions, not all uses of such clauses are in the proposition-specifying business; and the ones that specify reasons cannot be in that business at all, for otherwise they would subvert their own purpose.

The natural response to these considerations is to insist that it is not propositions as such that are good reasons, but true ones. This, however, does not make the right sort of difference. The argument was not that false propositions cannot be good reasons. It was based, not on thoughts about truth and falsehood, but on meta-physical considerations. If propositions are deemed incapable of being good reasons for action on the ground that they are too thin or insubstantial, or that they are the wrong sort of thing, true propo-sitions will be no better than false ones, since all will be equally inadequate to the task. A true proposition is the same sort of meta-physical beast as a false one.

There is of course a great difference between *the true proposi-tion that p* and *that the proposition that p is true* (which perhaps is the same as the truth of the proposition that *p*). The latter is a state of affairs, or at least it would be if it obtained (though there is also the true proposition that the proposition that *p* is true), and as such is indeed the right sort of thing to make an action right, though the situation in which it is really the truth of the proposition that *p* that makes the action right, rather than more simply that *p*, would cer-tainly be an unusual one.

I offer this argument as conclusive against the suggestion that a thing believed, understood as a proposition, is capable of being a normative reason. But I want to place that argument in a broader metaphysical context. In general there seems to me to be a great distinction between the sorts of thing that are capable of being the case and those that are capable of being true. Plantinga (1974) argues that a possible world is a maximal state of affairs, which may or may not obtain (only the actual world obtains). For each such world there is a set of propositions or *book* for that world, which things are true if the world obtains, each proposition being made true by a state of affairs that obtains or is the case there. Like Plantinga, I see an ontological gulf between things capable of being the case (i.e. states of affairs) and things capable of being true (either propositions or sentences). And only those capable of being the case are capable of being a good reason.

One consideration that supports this claim is that anything that has a truth value must be in some way representational, since for something to be true things must be as it represents them as being. But no representation can as such be a good reason for anything. The existence of the representation can be, and so can its having other features (such as lewdness, for instance), and so can its being the case that things are as here represented. But all these last things are states of affairs and not themselves representations of anything. No representation is the case, and no representation can be a good reason. (Being the case hovers between existing on the one side and being true on the other.)

So much for the reasons for saying that propositions are the wrong sorts of thing to be normative reasons, good reasons for acting in certain ways or for believing this rather than that. It follows from this that the content-based strategy will need to produce a new account of the contents of our beliefs—the things that we believe. This account, if it is to serve the purposes of the content-based approach, must offer as contents things capable of being good reasons. To do this, it must somehow understand contents as states of affairs, or as at least capable of being states of affairs. But this will require significant revisions in current views within the philosophy of mind, especially when we remember that belief-contents will need to be capable of failing to be the case as well as of succeeding in being the case.

We might think that all that is involved here is to adopt some form of externalism in the philosophy of mind. But that would not be right. What is wanted is externalistic in one sense and not in another. It is externalistic in the sense that in many cases the content of a mental state is to be conceived of as something that is itself non-mental, non-abstract: as unlike a proposition as could be. We are here thinking that aspects of the world ('how things are') can enter the mind as contents of mental states. To put it in a familiar slogan, what is believed can be what is the case. But our view is non-externalistic in another sense, since if what is believed is not the case, the belief does not for that reason lack content. This is different from the way in which true externalists conceive of things. With an externalist conception of a demonstrative thought, for instance, such as 'That coat is dirty', it is held that if the object supposedly demonstrated does not exist, there is nothing that is thought, nothing that the thinker of the thought is thinking, unless the thought turns out not to be demonstrative after all. By analogy, take a form of externalism that instead of talking about objects being parts of belief-contents talked of entire states of affairs as contents of beliefs. This view should presumably say that a false belief has no content, since there is no state of affairs that is its content, unless we can say that all false beliefs have a different sort of content from that enjoyed by (some of) the true ones. We are not here committed to anything of this sort, since we are understanding content as that which is believed, and understanding that which is believed as something capable of being the case, but not necessarily as something that is the case. For a false belief may still have content, and if the belief is false, what is believed is not the case, but the agent still believes something rather than nothing.

There is, however, a second way of running a content-based form of psychologism that is not vulnerable to these difficulties, because it does not identify the content of belief with that which is to be capable of being a good reason.[5] Motivating reasons, on this second version, are strictly speaking psychological states of the agent, whose direct objects are propositions; while normative reasons are states of affairs, things capable of being the case. So far, so standard. The twist comes with the next claim, that an agent's motivating reasons are good ones when their propositional objects *represent* (not *are*) genuine states of affairs that really provide good reason for performing the action in question. The idea is that the overlapping of normative and motivating reasons that is demanded by the normative constraint is achieved by use of the notion of representation. Good motivating reasons are ones that represent or reflect a state of affairs that genuinely makes the action performed sensible or reasonable or right, in the circumstances. So

---

[5] I owe my understanding of this alternative possibility to Jay Wallace, in whose terms I have given it.

though we admittedly fail to show that motivating reasons are capable of being good reasons, there is a sufficiently close relation between them and the normative to still any genuine philosophical unease.

My response to this version of the content-based strategy is that it simply awards itself the concept of a good motivating reason, without really doing anything to show that it makes sense. It awards itself this prize because, given the terms of the debate, it needs to do so if it is to show a good sense in which a motivating reason can enjoy a normative status and thus get close to meeting the normative constraint (which is all that it is trying to do). But the normative status it enjoys is that of being, not a good reason, but a good motivating reason. The only good reasons, according to this strategy, are states of affairs. Motivating reasons are good motivating reasons when they represent the things that are really good reasons. And we cannot turn a good motivating reason into a good reason by simply ignoring the little word 'motivating', since the strategy involves the admission that motivating reasons, being psychological states, can never be good reasons.

Now when I ask myself what one would naturally mean by talking of a good motivating reason, the answer seems to be one that one ought to be motivated by. But there are, according to this strategy, no such things as beliefs that one ought to be motivated by. It is states of affairs that ought to motivate us, not our own psychology.

Perhaps, however, the thought is merely that we can *call* 'good' any motivating reason that represents a state of affairs that is a good reason. But this does seem like awarding oneself the prize. The purpose of the normative constraint was to demand that motivating reasons be not excluded from the normative realm. We do not do much to meet that demand by finding a simple correlation between motivating reasons, conceived as stubbornly non-normative, and those states of affairs that do play a normative role.

My conclusion is that neither form of the appeal to content manages to reinstate a psychologistic conception of motivating reasons.

Psychologism, as we are understanding it, conceives of motivating reasons as psychological states, not as things expressible using that-clauses. The reason why I act will be my belief that p in the sense of my believing that p, not that I believe that p. Psychologism makes the mistake of interpreting our practice of reason-giving by saying such things as 'He did it because he believed that *p*' as adducing a *state* as the agent's reason. We are, as it were, driven from ordinary reason-giving in such terms as 'He did it because *p*' understood as 'He did it in the light of the fact that *p*', to specifications of his reason as 'He did it because he believed that *p*', and from there further to the view that this new specification adduces a psychological state as the agent's motivating reason. Having gone this far, it is impossible for psychologism to return on its tracks and announce that the agent's reason can be taken by the agent as a good reason—that the agent's reason can be conceived of as something in the light of which the action can appear to be right or sensible.

In this chapter I have argued against psychologism, the claim that all motivating reasons are psychological states of the agent. My general line has been that motivating reasons are not so far removed from the normative as psychologism leads us to suppose. Of course my attack on psychologism has done nothing directly to refute the rather different theory that insists that agent's reasons, motivating reasons, are more properly formulated as 'because he believes that *p*' than as simply 'that *p*'. This theory needs separate treatment, which it will receive next.

6

As I Believe

1. *Because he Believes that* p

If the reasons that motivate us are not psychological states of our-selves, our believings or belief-states, we might still feel that the things we believe cannot be those reasons either. The main reason for saying so is a worry about the case where things are not as the agent conceives them to be. Surely, in such a case, we cannot say that his reason for acting as he did was that *p*. We have to say that his reason for acting was that he believed that *p*. Accepting this for the case where the relevant belief is false, then, we might still hope that 'that *p*' can indeed be the explanation of the action where it is the case that *p*, but that where it is not the case that *p* the expla-nation can only be 'that he believed that *p*'. But, as Bernard Williams puts it (1980: 102), the true–false distinction should not be allowed to affect the form of the relevant explanation. Suppos-ing, therefore, that our explanation should take the same form whether it is or is not the case that *p*, and having already accepted that the correct explanation in cases where it is not the case that *p* is 'that he believed that *p*', we are driven to say the same where the relevant belief is true rather than false. We may of course allow that the simpler explanation 'that *p*' is not actually false or wrong as an explanation. But we suppose that, properly understood, it should be seen as enthymematic, i.e. as an acceptable shorthand version of the full explanation.

This new theory has one great advantage over psychologism. This is that it provides as reasons things that can be believed, things properly expressible using that-clauses. That I believe that *p* is something that can itself be believed and that is capable both of being the case and of not being the case. It therefore meets the con-straint sometimes put by demanding that all motivating reasons be propositional in form (Bond 1983: 22; Darwall 1983: 33). We have

seen worries about this, since we do not want to end up supposing
that good reasons are true propositions, or indeed propositions of
any sort. But by 'propositional in form' we need only take ourselves
to mean that a motivating reason must be capable of being
believed, asserted, doubted, supported, and so on, in the sorts of
ways that many philosophers have supposed that only propositions
can be.

Though it has this advantage over psychologism, the new theory
is very close to it. Indeed, some find it hard to distinguish between
the theory that holds that motivating reasons are psychological
states of the agent, conceived as believings, and the theory that
holds that they are such things as 'that the agent believes that *p*'.
The two theories unite in opposition to the view that motivating
reasons are things that the agent believes, which is the position I
am trying to defend. Because they are so close, we need to be sure
that they are genuinely distinct.

One important potential difference between them is that the
states which psychologism offers as motivating reasons are thought
of as static events, and so as capable of being causes of actions (also
conceived of as events). A psychological state understood in this
way can play this role of cause of action—cause of bodily movement, probably—without strain. Construed as a static event, it is
fitted to play its part in the relation commonly called 'event-
causation'—an extensional relation between particulars. That the
agent believes that *p*, by contrast, can only be conceived as a cause
of his subsequent action if we allow that that-clauses can specify
causes. If they do, and if the sort of cause that they specify is not
reducible to event-causation in some way, we are dealing with the
sort of causation sometimes called 'fact-causation', though whether
the thing specified by the that-clause is a fact or a state of affairs
seems to be a matter of debate. However that may be, it remains
the case that if there is a difference between fact-causation and
event-causation, there is the same difference between our two
theories.

There are of course other differences. The mental state can be
interrupted; that I believe that *p* cannot. The mental state, understood as a static event, occurs; that I believe that *p* obtains, or is the
case. The mental state has some sort of location; that I believe that
p does not. The mental state is at least potentially identifiable with
a neural state, and may be conceived as a functional state. That I

believe that *p* cannot be conceived functionally, nor can it possibly be identified with a neural state of any sort. It is quite the wrong sort of thing for that.[1]

Consider the difference between my nervousness, which is a mental state, and that I am nervous, which is not. My nervousness may explain my jumping whenever there is a loud noise; that I am nervous explains why I take beta-blockers when I have to sing in public, since my reason for doing so is that I am nervous, while my nervousness is not my reason for jumping at loud noises. (In fact I don't do this for a reason at all.) So explanations that appeal to mental states as *explanantia* are not equivalent to explanations that appeal to such things as 'that the agent is in such-and-such a mental state'.

It seems then that the new theory, as a theory of motivating reasons, is genuinely distinct from psychologism. We should also note that various arguments, often offered as arguments in favour of psychologism, are really only arguments in favour of the new theory. We saw one of these in the previous chapter:

The statement

(1) *A*'s reason for φ-ing was that *p*

can only be true if

(2) *A* believed that *p*.

Therefore

(3) *A*'s reason for φ-ing was (*really*) that *A* believed that *p*.

There is also the argument mentioned above, that if it is not the case that *p*, we are forced to understand the reason why the agent acted as 'that he believed that *p*' *rather than* as the simpler 'that *p*'. We then infer that we must say the same sort of thing of all cases, including those where the agent is not wrong about whether it is the case that *p*.

---

[1] One could go further than I do in the text and suggest that the understanding of beliefs and desires as psychological states is a philosophical confusion. Helen Steward (1997) argues persuasively that the conception of beliefs and desires as psychological states illegitimately converts facts (that he believes that *p*) into states of the agent (his believing that *p*), in ways intended to support an understanding of action-explanation in terms of event-causation, and also to make possible an identification of states of mind with states of the brain. (See also the writings cited in Ch. 5 n. 3.) I view this as an internecine debate between supporters of two theories both of which I reject. Steward ends up supporting a form of what I am calling here the 'new theory'.

These two arguments raise questions that need to be answered. The first asks what role we are to attribute to the fact that the agent believed that *p* in cases where we none the less want to explain the action by appeal to the simpler 'that *p*'. I will address this question in the next section. The second asks about the relation between cases where it is, and where it is not, the case that *p*. Can the simpler explanation 'that *p*' be run in cases where it is not the case that *p*? I address this in Section 3 below.

So these arguments do need to be addressed, and I will address them. But still their conclusion is false, and can be shown to be false. The crucial point is this. There are indeed cases in which (1) gets the agent's reason wrong and (3) gets it right, but these are rather unusual, and the way in which they are unusual reveals the falsehood of the new theory as a general view about reasons and motivation. Consider a case where my reason for acting is genuinely that I believe that *p*. For instance, that I believe that the cliff is crumbling is my reason for avoiding climbing it, because having that belief I am more likely to fall off (I will get nervous). This is a case where that I believe what I do is genuinely my reason for action, in a way that is independent of whether the belief is actually true. As I might say, whether the cliff actually is crumbling or not doesn't matter. I believe that it is crumbling, and this alone is sufficient to motivate me to stay away from it. I recognize that if the cliff were not crumbling, I would still have just the same reason not to climb it as if it were, so long as I continue to believe it to be crumbling. But this is a quite unusual situation, not at all the normal case.[2] Normally, I suppose that if things are not as I believe them to be, I do not in fact have the reason that I take myself to have. It would be quite peculiar to suppose that no practical reasons are like this, and that all are of the special sort that we found in the case of the crumbly cliff.

The suggestion here is that we determine what our reason is by considering what it varies with. If the reason remains when the supposed ground for it vanishes, that supposed ground was not the actual ground. Normally we take our reasons to be grounded in objective features of the situation, and to disappear if those features disappear. If my reason for not climbing had been that the

---

[2] I have borrowed this form of argument from Joseph Raz (1986: 142–3). A different and maybe better example would be where what motivates me not to climb the cliff is that I believe that I can't climb it.

cliff was crumbly, that is how I would have been thinking of things; I would have supposed my reason to persist until the cliff ceases to be crumbly. But in the case of the example as I have given it, I know that my reason for not climbing persists *as long as I continue to believe* that the cliff is crumbly. This is how I conceive of my own reason. So this is genuinely a case where it is 'that I believe that *p*' that is my reason for action.

There are other such cases once one begins to look for them. Someone who believes that there are pink rats living in his shoes may take that he believes this as a reason to go to the doctor or perhaps a psychoanalyst. This is quite different from the person who takes (his belief) that there are pink rats living in his shoes as a reason to call in the pest control officer.[3] Such contrasts show that we will distort what we have been calling the light in which the agent acted, or the agent's reasons, if we insist that they are properly specified as 'that he believed that *p*'. If there is a significant difference between the explanation 'that he believed that *p*' and the simpler 'that *p*', the advantage is normally all on the side of the simpler version. 'That I believe that *p*' is almost never the right way to specify the light in which I act, my reasons for doing what I do, if it is taken as significantly different from the simpler 'that *p*'.

The form of argument that I have been using here is unusual, but surely none the worse for that. It involves showing, of some supposedly general thesis, that the situations of which it is most obviously true are very uncommon ones (and in the present case necessarily so), so that the general thesis must be false as a general thesis *just because* of the peculiar nature of the cases which it correctly characterizes.

So the 'new theory' is false, and false for different reasons from those that toppled psychologism. Of course it is not common to see psychologism distinguished from the new theory in the way that I have done. And this offers an advantage to those who think, more generally, that the explanation of action must somehow hinge on reference to the agent's beliefs. My suspicion is that the strengths of each view have been falsely claimed by the other, while the objections to each view are avoided by the other, so that the ability to flit from one view to the other (failing to see the difference between them) is a great advantage. Arguments from naturalism

[3] I owe this sort of example to John Hyman.

and from the need for the explanation of action to be causal suit psychologism better than they suit the new theory. Arguments from the need for belief and the possibility of error are really arguments for the new theory in the first instance. Equally, the objections I raised to psychologism do not apply to the new theory, and vice versa.

None of this means that we can just dismiss the arguments offered in support of the new theory. As I have already said, those arguments raise questions that need to be addressed. I now turn to consider the first of those arguments. How should we explain the fact that, where the agent's reason for acting is that *p*, the agent must believe that *p*, if not by saying that the agent's reason for acting is 'really' that he believes that *p*?

2. *The Role of Belief in the Psychologizing Restatement of a Reason*

Whenever the agent acts in the light of the fact that *p*, the agent must take it that *p*, and I understand this sort of 'taking it that' as a weak form of belief. And ordinarily, we have claimed, the psychologized explanation of the action is to be understood as the same explanation as the non-psychologized one. Sometimes the psychologized explanation is inappropriate, even misleading. The opportunities for use of the explanation 'I am doing this because I think I am married' are rare, one might say; to use this form of words definitely gives one to understand that there is something odd about the situation (as if one might not be quite sure whether the divorce had come through). None the less, if I act in the light of the fact that I am married, I must believe that I am. So what role does 'that I believe I am married' play in the explanation? It seems as if the belief must be there but is not allowed to make much of a contribution, and this is very odd. So what role can the normative story assign to the belief?

Collins's view is that I insert an 'I believe that' into the explanation of my action (actual or intended) when I am in some doubt about whether I am right; the phrase signals that uncertainty. Equally, in the third-person case we move to the psychologized explanation when we take it that the matter is dubious or that the agent is mistaken. In the first-person case, the transaction as a whole is to be understood in terms of a Gricean conversational implicature. The implication of uncertainty can be cancelled, as when one says, perhaps, 'The reason why I am going to do it is that I believe that p, though I have to say that I am not in any doubt about the matter'. There is clearly much truth in this, but it seems to me not to be an answer to our question. The question is not one about when we do and when we don't adopt the psychologized form of explanation. It is about the role of the belief in the story as a whole if it is not playing the focal role normally attributed to it.

What other account of the role of belief is available to the normative story? I can think of two. The first involves a structural distinction in the theory of explanation. There is a difference between a consideration that is a proper part of an explanation, and a consideration that is required for the explanation to go through, but which is not itself a part of that explanation. I call the latter 'enabling conditions'. For instance, that England is not sinking beneath the waves today is a consideration in the absence of which what explains my actions would be incapable of doing so. But that does nothing to show that England's not submerging today is part of the explanation of why I do what I do (or more generally of my doing what I do). It is therefore an enabling condition in this case, though of course it is a proper part of the explanation of some other things, for instance of why the ports are not disappearing under water. The suggestion therefore is that the believing, conceived traditionally as a psychological state, is an enabling condition for an explanation which explains the action in terms of the reasons for (i.e. in favour of—the good reasons for) doing it. This condition is required for that explanation to go through. That is, in the absence of the believing, what in fact explains the action would not then explain it, either because the action would not then have been done at all, or because, if it had, it would have been done for another reason and so been explained in another way. But the believing does not contribute directly to the explanation.

The difficulty that I see with this move is not so much that the notion of an enabling condition requires theoretical support that I have not provided here. It is rather that there is no clear account of where the line that it draws is to come, case by case. It is not clear what one is to say to someone who insists that the believing is a proper part of the explanation. And so we can have no confidence that there won't be plenty of occasions in which the believing will end up within the explanation rather than outside it, returning us to our starting-point.

I have something of a reply to this point, which is that the appeal to enabling conditions is made after we have established that motivating reasons must be able to be normative ones, to be good reasons, and shown therefore that motivating reasons do not standardly include psychological states of the agent.[4] It is also made after we have established that explanations of the form 'that I believe that *p*' are not normally the correct way of specifying the light in which I act, if they are conceived of as distinct in style from the simpler explanation they are intended to replace. Having got this far, however, we have a principled reason for insisting that the believing, or that the agent so believed, is not to be taken as a proper part of the relevant explanation. We were looking for a way of recognizing the fact that it is never wrong to admit a reference to the agent's belief in the story; we can do this, consistently with the results we have already accepted, only by allowing that the believing, or that the agent believes, counts as an enabling condition rather than as a part of the motivating reason. We could not, for instance, say that the believing is part of the motivating reason, the rest being constituted by the normative reason. For this would return us to the point that the (now complex) motivating reason is incapable of being the normative reason. Nor could we say that 'that the agent believes that *p*' is really the agent's reason, or among the agent's reasons; for to insist on this would be to distort our account of the light in which the agent acted. So there is a principled explanation of the fact that the believing must be seen as an enabling condition rather than as a proper part of the explanation on each occasion.

However, I do not feel confident enough in this reply to rely on it entirely. This motivates me to look for another account of the reference to belief in 'He is doing it because he believes that *p*'. The one that appeals to me is what I call the appositional account. This hears 'He is doing it because he believes that *p*' as 'He is doing

[4] In correspondence, Arthur Collins glosses this remark as the thought that an enabling condition cannot be assimilated by the explanation because it is only pertinent in light of the antecedent recognition of the potential validity of the explanation.

it because p, as he believes'. The 'as he believes' functions paratactically here, attaching itself to the 'p'. Again, it is not part of the specification of his reason, but is a comment on that reason, one that is required by the nature of the explanation that we are giving. That explanation specifies the features *in the light of which* the agent acted. It is required for this sort of explanation that those features be present to the agent's consciousness—indeed, that they be somehow conceived as favouring the action; so there must always be a way of making room for this fact, in some relation to the explanation that runs from features as reasons to action as response. It is not required, however, that the nature of the agent's consciousness itself either constitute, or even be part of, the *explanans*. The appositional account tells us how to hold all these things together in a coherent whole.

More needs to be said about this paratactic comment. How, for instance, are we to understand statements like 'If I had not believed that p, I would not have done it'? Is there any possibility of running some paraphrase such as 'If it had not been the case, as I believed, that p, I would not have done it'? This seems strained to me, at best; on its most natural hearing, it sounds equivalent to 'If it had not been the case that p, I would not have done it', which is not at all what we want. But we are not here in the business of contributing to the famous Davidsonian research programme. There is perhaps a harder question whether we can, understanding the phrase 'I believe that p' appositionally, retain the validity of *modus ponens* and other inference schemata. In general, however, I offer the appositional account as a philosophical explication of the sense of 'I believe that p', rather than as a contribution to formal philosophy of language. It is only if it is taken in the latter way that these hard-edged questions get a bite.

There are interesting questions here about the relation between the appositional account and the enabling conditions account. One view is that they are distinct. For the enabling conditions account may seem to be committed to the existence of the belief as a psychological state, while the appositional account is consistent with the more radical suggestion that belief is more a stance or commitment than a state. The appositional account, that is, leaves it open what sort of philosophical story we should tell about belief, in a way that the enabling condition account does not. So the appositional account enjoys a considerable strategical advantage, and we should adopt it in preference to the enabling conditions account.

Still, we can never deny that the agent believes that p, if we once explain his action by saying that he did it for the reason that p, as he supposes. Indeed, as I see it, the two sentences at issue:

> His reason for doing it was that p, as he supposed
> His reason for doing it was that he supposed that p

entail each other.[5] What is more, the second of them is to be understood as entailing that the agent supposed or believed that p. So on either account, appositional or enabling conditions, we have to allow that, had the agent not believed that p, he could not have acted for the reason that p. And this is really all that it amounts to to say that his belief that p is an enabling condition for his acting for the reason that p. What is more, if there is sufficient reason to deny that belief is a psychological state, that reason must be compatible with some positive account of what is going on in ordinary belief-attributions. It is not as if we are forced to allow that the reference to belief in the appositional clause is a reference to a psychological state, just because the appositional clause entails the straightforward claim that the agent believed that p. So perhaps the correct view is that there are two versions of the enabling condition account, one that takes the belief as a psychological state and the other that does not. The appositional version of things is not committed to either version as such.

Why not just say that what explains the action is that p and that the agent believed that p? Because this just opens the door for those who want to argue that the 'that p' is redundant—for in cases where what the agent believes is not the case, we just drop the first conjunct without our explanation being at all damaged or diminished thereby. And we have already seen that this is wrong. Psychologized explanations give the wrong explanation of action, if we conceive of them as somehow preferable to the simpler non-psychologized ones. That the agent believed that p is not the sole correct explanation of the action, even in a case where the belief was false.

---

[5] Except in the special sorts of case discussed in Sect. 1 above.

3. *Factive and Non-Factive Explanations*

The previous section concerned the difficulties thought to arise because of the universal insertability of the 'I believe that', and the admission that if the agent does not believe that p, his reason for acting cannot be that p. This new section concerns the relevance of the claim that, if it is not the case that p, the reason why the agent acted cannot be that p and *must* be that he believed that p. The case of the false belief, as we might put it, drives a wedge between the psychologized and the non-psychologized explanation, in favour of the former. And once this point has been made about cases where the relevant belief is false, we will have to say the same thing about cases where it is true. For we are allowing that the true–false distinction should not affect the form of the relevant explanation.

It is at this point that we return to matters raised early in Chapter 1. I originally distinguished between the reasons why we do what we do and the good reasons for acting in that way. But I suggested (in 1.2) that explanation of action in terms of the reasons that motivated the agent is only one way of explaining why the agent did what he did. All explanations can be given in terms of reasons, after all, even those that are not explanations of action. We can ask for the reason why the sun goes down the sky towards evening, even though we know perfectly well that the sun does not do this for a reason of its own, as it were. We are not, impossibly, supposing that the trajectory of the sun is something intentionally chosen by the sun in the light of these and those considerations. Even when we restrict ourselves to the explanation of intentional action, which will still be offered in terms of reasons, we need not always suppose that the reasons we offer in explanation of why the agent did what he did are among what we have been calling 'the agent's reasons', or that the agent acted in the light of those reasons. Explaining in terms of the reasons that motivated the agent is a special case of explaining (giving the reason) why he acted as he did.

Now one form of pressure in favour of the psychologized explanation of intentional action derives from the simple thought that all explanation is factive. What this means is that from an explanation of the form 'The reason why it is the case that p is that q' we can infer both that p and that q. This is no different from the relation between 'He knows that p' and 'p', or between 'He has

forgotten that *p*' and '*p*'. For him to know that *p* or to have forgotten that *p* or indeed to have remembered that *p*, it must be the
case that *p*. In this sense, we say that knowledge and remembering
are factive; and so is forgetting. Equally, various locutions in which
we characteristically give explanations are factive. As I said above,
'The reason why it is the case that *p* is that *q*' is doubly factive,
entailing both that *p* and that *q*. So is 'The explanation of its being
the case that *p* is that *q*'. The question then arises whether all explanations are factive in this sense. Suppose that my question 'What
were his reasons for doing that?' is a request for explanation, and
that the explanation can be given by laying out the considerations
in the light of which he determined to do what he did. Suppose also
that, in those considerations, the agent was mistaken. Things were
not as he supposed them to be in relevant respects. Does this mean
that we cannot base our explanation on those considerations? Is
explanation in terms of motivating reasons always factive, like
other explanation, or is it non-factive? If it is non-factive, it is different from other sorts of explanation. But we should not beg the
question by assuming that such a thing is impossible, though no
doubt it will affect our general conception of explanation should
things so turn out. The question, then, is whether there is a way of
explaining an action by laying out the considerations in the light of
which the agent acted without committing ourselves to things being
as the agent there conceived them to be.

I take it that the answer to this question is yes. I suggest that locutions such as

> His reason for doing it was that it would increase his pension
> The ground on which he acted was that she had lied to him

are not factive. To test this, we only need to consider whether it is
possible without contradiction to continue by denying that things
were as the agent took them to be. Consider the following
sentences:

> His reason for doing it was that it would increase his pension,
> but in fact he was quite wrong about that.

> The ground on which he acted was that she had lied to him,
> though actually she had done nothing of the sort.

Neither of these sentences sounds self-contradictory to me. Not
everyone's ears agree with me about this, I know. But there seems

to be no reason why there should not be a way of revealing the light in which the agent saw things as a way of explaining why he did what he did, but without asserting that he was right to see things that way. I think that the two locutions above are ways of doing that. They are not, of course, the only ways of doing it. We can achieve the same thing by saying:

> He did it because he took it that it would increase his pension.
>
> What explains his doing it was that he thought it would increase his pension.
>
> The reason why he did it was that he fondly imagined that it would increase his pension.
>
> He did it for the reason that, as he imagined, it would increase his pension.
>
> He did this because, as he supposed, she had lied to him.

In the first two of these five cases, we have apparently recognized the factive nature of the locution we are using, in offering after the 'because' and 'explains' a sentence that is true. The same is true of the third. In the last two cases, matters are a little more delicate. Suppose that she had not lied to him, but that he thought that she had. Is it true that, as he supposed, she had lied to him? No. It is not quite clear what truth value this sentence now has, but it does seem clear that it does not have the truth value true. So the insertion of the apposition 'as he believed' does not take us from a falsehood to a truth in the way that the insertion of 'he believed that . . .' does, or at least can do. What it does is to remove the speaker's commitment to things being as the agent supposed. So the appositional use is a sort of halfway house. The relevant context is not factive, since any commitment to the truth of the contained clause can be removed without incoherence, but it has something of the style of a factive explanation, for if you take the apposition out, there is a strong *suggestio veri*.

It may be that there are some forms of action-explanation that are factive and some that are not. I see no need to decide this issue; my main point is that the purposes of explanation of action in terms of the agent's reasons do not require such explanation to be factive. (Do we, for instance, find forms of inference to the best explanation at all tempting in this case?) Where we are dealing with a non-factive form, there is no real need to include the apposition in order to avoid commitment to things being as the agent supposed. If the explanation is not factive, it is not factive. Any commitment there may be will be more in the style of a conversational implicature than an entailment. So we might want to include the apposition in order to guard ourselves against the implicature otherwise carried by some forms of explanation, that the agent was right about the matter. Some hear 'He did this because she had lied to him' as factive, and so as the wrong explanation of his action if she had not lied to him. Others hear it as carrying a *suggestio veri*, but a cancellable one, so that where the agent is mistaken, we can still explain his action by saying 'He did this because, as he supposed, she had lied to him'. And this pattern of choices repeats with the other styles that our action-explanation can take, e.g. 'His reason for doing this was that p'.

What conclusions can we draw from all this? The most general conclusion is in line with what was claimed in Chapter 1.2: that there are explanations of action that do not succeed simply by laying out the agent's reasons for action in the terms that the agent would have done if asked. Restricting ourselves now to attempts to specify the agent's reasons, in the sense that we have given to that phrase, we have decided that though some such attempts may involve a factive context, others do not. The ones that do not are ones that involve a contained intensional context, such as that introduced by 'he believes that . . .', so that the whole can be true *as an explanation*, though the contained part, the thing doing the explaining, is not. There are, then, both factive and non-factive ways of laying out the considerations in the light of which the agent acted.

If this is so, it seems to me that the difference between the factive and the non-factive cannot be of any real significance when it comes to the explanation of action. We can phrase our explanation as we like, and that is the end of the matter. So it cannot be that the very notion of explanation drives us to the use of the phrase 'because he believed that . . .' in order to live up to the factive demands associated with the explanation of events. In this sense, a thing believed that is not the case can still explain an action.

It follows from this that if we do decide to use the factive turn of phrase in giving our explanation of his action, this cannot be because we are driven by the need to find a factive explanation. We do not need to do this, and there are available plenty of effectively equivalent turns of phrase that would have enabled us to do things differently. If the agent's conception of the situation is mistaken, there are some ways of explaining his action that are now ruled out. But this does not show that only factive ones are left in, forcing us towards the phrasing 'He did it because he believed that *p*'. If we do use the factive ones, this will be a comparatively arbitrary choice.

The picture that is emerging here is one that is very congenial to Collins's basic point: for the agent the psychologized and the non-psychologized explanations are effectively equivalent. We tend to suppose that, once we move to the third-person perspective, things are very different in this respect, on the grounds that the purposes of explanation force us to move to a *different* explanation of the action—one whose general structure consists in a relation between the action and the psychology of the agent *rather than* in a relation between the action and the light in which the agent saw it. But this is a distortion of what is going on when we move from one form of explanation to the other. The distinction between first and third person does not allow us to suppose that in the third-person case, there is a radical distinction between the psychologized and the non-psychologized forms of explanation, when there is no such radical difference in the first-person case. There is only one sort of explanation, though the form in which we may choose to give that explanation may vary according to the circumstances. What is more, the most revealing form, perhaps I should say, the form least likely to mislead philosophers, is the simple form which contains no visible reference to belief at all.

I close this section with a summary of the position so far, and an analogy. The fact that the agent would not have performed the action had he not believed that *p* should not persuade us that the proper way of specifying the reason in the light of which he acted was as 'that he believed that *p*'. This sort of counterfactual test takes us in the wrong direction, since it invites us to ignore the differences between two relations: first, the special relation that holds between the reason for which the action was done and the action done for that reason, and second the more general relation that holds between the action and any other condition in the absence of which it would not have been done for the reason that it was. And anyway, there are examples that show the need to distinguish between those special cases of reasons that involve the agent's belief and those that don't. The counterfactual test invites us to blur that distinction. One may feel some unease about saying 'His reason was that *p*' when we don't ourselves believe that *p*. But this too should not drive us to saying 'His reason was that he believed that *p*', supposing that by this device we are respecting the factive nature of explanation; we can avoid any apparent commitment on our part to things being as the agent supposed by use of one of a number of special constructions such as 'as he supposed'.

The analogy that follows I owe to Lloyd Humberstone, and I give it largely in his words. Let us think of what we might call the 'grounds' for a punishment, where the notion of a ground is being used stipulatively for whatever fills the for-phrase in such sentences as 'He was sentenced to six years for armed robbery'. In crime fiction, or in talk-back radio from callers who pride themselves on a certain kind of cynicism, one sometimes hears people say such things as 'Nobody ever got sent to prison for robbing banks, only for getting caught robbing banks'. This can be thought of as another misinvocation of the counterfactual test. The idea is that since you wouldn't be sentenced to imprisonment unless you had been caught, what you are being sentenced for is: having been caught. There would be a similar mistake if being convicted were cited instead of being caught as (what we are calling) the grounds for punishment. What we want to say is that the prisoner is serving time for robbing a bank, rather than for being caught (etc.). But what happens when we think the prisoner has been wrongly convicted, or even when we just don't want to commit ourselves to the correctness of the conviction, because of the factive ring to 'He is serving ten years for robbing a bank'? In these cases we need a decommitment operator, which normally amounts to slipping in the word 'allegedly' before 'robbing a bank', in appositional style. There is indeed no offence of allegedly robbing a bank, and one cannot be accused of that, nor convicted of it. But one can be punished for it, and put in prison for it, in a sense. The explanation of this is that there is no factive pull in the notion of accusation, nor in that of conviction, but there is in the notion of 'punishment for'.

It seems, then, that the explanation of action, at least that of intentional action, can always be achieved by laying out the considerations in the light of which the agent saw the action as desirable, sensible, or required. If things were as the agent supposed, there is no bar against the agent's reasons being among the reasons in favour of doing what he actually did. That is to say, the reasons that motivated the agent can be among or even identical with the good reasons in the case, those that favour acting as he did. Equally, the good reasons can motivate him, since they can be the considerations in the light of which he acted, and citing them can explain the action directly rather than only being able to do so indirectly as part of the content of a suitable psychological state. Good reasons explain action in any case where the agent chose to do that action in the light of those reasons. The psychological state that the agent is in is not, of course, simply irrelevant to the explanation. But neither is it the focus of that explanation. Equally, that the agent has the relevant beliefs is not irrelevant, but is not the focus of the explanation either.

One contentious aspect of the picture that has been developed here is that something that is not the case can explain an action. Another is that a normative fact (for instance, that I owe it to her to do what she asks) can explain an action. Explanations by appeal to the normative or to the non-obtaining are not what we are used to. Nor, even, are we used to the idea that a simple matter of fact can explain an action; we are too used to hearing about beliefs and desires. But these things are things that I think we should countenance without too much reluctance. In doing so, we will be giving one sense to the idea that reality is practical. The reasons that motivate us can be things that are the case.

The other sense to the idea that reality is practical is that good reasons can be, or be grounded in, considerations other than those concerning the psychology of the agent. Here I have especially in mind the desires of the agent. If, as I argued in Chapters 2 and 3, few if any reasons are either desire-based or belief-based, we are a long way towards establishing on the normative side too that reality can be practical. Features of our surroundings can be, or at least can give us, reasons in favour of acting in one way rather than another.

7

Consequential Matters

1. *Disjunctive Conceptions*

In the previous chapter I argued against one view and in favour of another. The view I argued against was the view that all explanations of action should properly be of the form '*A* acted because he believed that *p*'. The view I supported was effectively that there is no significant difference between explanations of that form and those of the simpler form '*A* acted for the reason that *p*'; or that, if there is a difference, the philosophical advantages lie on the side of the simpler form.

The two views at issue agreed on one point. Neither involved any breach of the explanatory maxim that the true–false distinction should not be allowed to affect the form of the relevant explanation. In broad brush, I argued that we should take our lead from the form of explanation appropriate when things are going well, i.e. when things are effectively as the agent supposes them to be. My opponent argued the opposite: that we should be driven here by the form of explanation that is appropriate when things are not going well, and understand in those terms the case where things are going better. This was what drove the view that, since on some occasions we must use the phrasing 'because the agent believed that' in explaining the action, we must use it on all occasions. This view was supposedly forced on us by the combination of two elements. The first was the nature of cases where things are not as the agent supposed. The second was the explanatory maxim.

I disputed my opponent's understanding of the unsuccessful case, arguing that the explanation of action is not factive, and that we therefore do not need to explain such actions using an *explanans* that is the case. Now, since the explanatory maxim is proving so influential in this debate, it is time to subject it to some sort of critical examination. I want to suggest that in fact it has fewer teeth than may so far have appeared.

It is a commonplace to remark that the debate about the explanation of action bears notable similarities to that about the nature of perceptual states, especially that aspect which revolves around the rights and wrongs of the infamous Argument from Illusion.[1] There are two significant features of the Argument from Illusion that are relevant for our purposes here. The first has already appeared. It is that those who wield the Argument take it that the nature of the unsuccessful case is capable of determining how we should describe the successful case. Perceptual success is to be understood as what is present when there is perceptual failure (illusion, delusion, hallucination) *plus* some added extra such as a suitable cause or a good fit between perceptual state and world. There is a basic element common to veridical perception and illusion; we get veridical perception when that common element is graced by a further, quite independent element whose presence is not determined by that of the common one. The common element can be understood in terms to which success is incidental.

What drives this insistence that success = [failure + added ingredient] is an appeal to indistinguishability. The fact that the perceiver cannot distinguish (from inside, as it were) the case of success (genuine perception) from that of failure (illusion) weights the scales in favour of a 'highest common factor' account of the situation. For by far the smoothest way of accounting for the indistinguishability is that of showing that so far as the surface of things goes, we are dealing with the very same thing both times.

In my 'Arguments from Illusion' (1995b) I suggested that this pattern of argumentation is quite common, being found in various quite different areas of philosophy. I found examples in the philosophy of action (in the relation between acting and trying to act), in epistemology (in the relation between knowledge and belief), and, crucially, in the debate about what it is to act for a reason. And I go on to discuss how to respond to such arguments. But in no case do I suppose that they are successful.

In the previous chapter, however, I seem to have forgotten all about this. For I appear to use an indistinguishability argument (taken largely from Collins), and I argue for a highest common

---

[1] See e.g. Dancy (1995b) and Stout (1996: 26 ff.).

factor conception of acting for or in the light of a reason, to which success is an indifferent extra. That things are as he takes them to be is not itself required for the success of my explanation of his action in terms of the light in which he saw the situation. Success here is an added extra, one quite independent of the presence of all the elements necessary for an effective explanation.

This combination of features is absolutely characteristic of an argument from illusion. It was also common ground between my opponent and me. We were both impressed by the relevant indistinguishability, and we were both conceiving of success as highest common factor + added ingredient. The only argument between us was whether to understand success in terms of failure or the other way round. The pressure on me was the normal pressure, once one has got that far, to let failure lead in the analysis.

What did not emerge at all was that there is a standard response to arguments from illusion, whatever their subject-matter. This response, which is equally relevant to the present case, is that of adopting a disjunctive conception of the relevant subject-matter. Such a conception is available in the present case. It would run something like this:

A φ-s for the reason that p iff

either p and that *p* is a reason for *φ-ing* and *A φ-s* in the light of the fact that *p*

or it is not the case that *p*, but *A* takes it that that *p* is a reason for *φ-ing*, and *A φ-s* in the light of his belief that *p*

or p, but that *p* is not a reason for *φ-ing* but *A* takes it that that *p* is a reason for *φ-ing*, and *A φ-s* in the light of the fact that *p*.

The relevance of this is that it explicitly renounces any attempt to provide a 'highest common factor' conception of acting for a reason. The indistinguishability at issue, i.e. the fact that from inside the agent cannot tell which of the three 'disjuncts' he is occupying, is catered for elsewhere in the full story. For instance, it could be catered for by seeing the three-part disjunction given above as a way of filling out the following less revealing, but still supposedly correct, disjunctive account:

A does x for the reason that p iff

either (1) *p* and that *p* is a reason for *φ-ing* and *A φ-s* in the light of the fact that *p*

or (2) it is for *A* as if (1) were the case.

What the availability of this disjunction shows, supposedly, is that there is a sense in which the successful case is dominant; the unsuccessful case(s) must be understood in terms of the successful one, in a way that means that if the successful case, as here understood, involved some incoherence, this incoherence would infect the unsuccessful too. Crucially, however, what we see here is that there can be more than one way in which (2) can come about—more than one type of unsuccessful case. The second two disjuncts given in the fuller account above specify two such ways. There may even be more; the disjunctive conception is neutral on the number of ways in which the *intelligendum* (or, worse, *definiendum*) can be realized.

The question for me, then, is why we should adopt a 'highest common factor' conception of acting for a reason, with its consequent vulnerability to the nature of the unsuccessful case, rather than a disjunctive conception, which suffers from no such vulnerability. Why don't we just say that the explanation of an action in cases where the agent is in error or confused is of a different style from that appropriate where there is no such defect, and point to the possibility of a disjunctive conception to justify our failure to insist on the same style of explanation throughout, as the explanatory maxim requires?

There is one particular advantage in adopting the disjunctive conception of acting for a reason. This is that it enables us to find a suitable way of understanding what goes on when someone acts in the light of a consideration that they wrongly take to be a reason in favour of what they are doing. For some people, even that characterization of what is going on in such a case is unsatisfactory, because they take the 'in the light of' relation, not as factive, necessarily (since one can act in the light of a consideration that is not the case, as I argued in the previous chapter), but as success-related in the sense that the consideration in the light of which one acts must be one that, had it been true, would indeed have counted in favour of doing what one did. To say of someone, then, that he acted in the light of a reason that is no reason is paradoxical, according to some. Such people can use the disjunctive account to express their position in a way that does not bind them to the view that *all* motivating reasons should be expressed in the form 'because the agent believed that *p*'. They can point out that, on the disjunctive conception, there are two distinct uses of 'in the light of'. The first disjunct contains the first use ('in the light of the fact that *p*'), while the second disjunct contains the second use ('in the light of *A*'s belief that *p*'). The first use is success-related in the sense given above, and the second is not. So it is indeed paradoxical to describe someone as acting for a reason that is no reason. We should instead have said that they acted in the light of a belief that is no reason.

By contrast, the position that I tried to defend in the previous chapter is committed to the offending formulation 'in the light of a reason that is no reason'. For it wants to hold that, in such a case, it is not as if the agent acts for no reason at all, though any belief of the agent is not the right sort of thing to be that in the light of which the agent acted; and it also allows that the reason for which the agent acted is not a good reason in favour of so acting. The combination of these two views leads to the offending result.

The phrase 'in the light of a belief that is no reason' is available to those who accept the view I attacked in the previous chapter, but only at the cost of expressing all motivating reasons in the form 'because the agent believed that *p*'. So, it might be said, this is a further incentive for me to adopt the disjunctive conception rather than the fully normative conception that I in fact defended. I can do this while retaining what is distinctive of my position, namely that it is possible to be motivated by a good reason. What distinguishes my original position from that of the disjunctivists is that, for me, *all* motivating reasons must be capable of being good reasons; disjunctivists assert such a thing only of the reasons captured in the first and third disjuncts. With the second disjunct, that which motivates the agent is not the right sort of thing to be a good reason for acting, or a reason that favours the action done, since it is a belief of the agent's rather than the thing believed.

Finally, it may look as if those who adopt the disjunctive conception of acting for a reason have explicitly renounced adherence to the explanatory maxim that the true–false distinction should not affect the form of the relevant explanation. For they appear to be saying quite different things about cases where things are as the agent supposes them to be and other cases, since they cope with these different sorts of case by means of different disjuncts. This last complaint, however, rests on an illusion, and it is important to see that this is so. For if we get the right *intelligendum*, i.e. the one given above, we can say that when *A* acts, the relevant explanation of his action will have the same form whether we are dealing with the true or the false. For in either case we will account for his action in terms of the reasons for which he acted. That we give a disjunctive conception of *this*, i.e. that things begin to diverge from here on, involves no rejection of the explanatory maxim. After all, at some point there will have to be a difference in the explanation we offer; so why not here? In sum, the explanatory maxim has no real teeth; the disjunctive conception can flout it at one level and still be held not to be in breach of it at another.

In reply to these complaints I first want to argue that any appeal to indistinguishability that I may have made, following the lead of Collins, is quite different from such appeals made in arguments from illusion. The need to give a rather similar account of the two styles of explanation was not based on the fact that the agent cannot tell the difference between them, as in the perceptual version of the Argument from Illusion. There is no reason to rely on the agent particularly here. It is not as if the agent is in some position of authority. We are dealing with a topic that is very different from the question how things appear to the agent, namely the appropriate explanation of the agent's action. Agents do not enjoy privileged access to such matters, even though they may enjoy privileged access to such things as what it is that they currently believe (i.e. how the world is, according to them) or the nature of their current perceptual experience. There are independent reasons for supposing that the agent is right to suppose that the psychologized and the non-psychologized explanation are the same explanation at bottom. Essentially, the agent is correct to take the psychologized restatement of an original reasons-explanation as just a more cautious version of the non-psychologized original. It is the same explanation both times, but the manner of its presentation differs. There is no reason for the agent to accept that the shift to the psychologized restatement of his reason either changes the subject-matter of the explanation or involves an attempt to specify something that the agent is somehow less likely to be wrong about. And since there is no reason for him to do that, there is no reason for us to do it either.

Second, the sense in which success is an indifferent extra to what is present in the case of failure (failure meaning that one of the disjuncts other than the first one is satisfied) is different here from what we get in standard examples of arguments from illusion. In the case that concerns us here, success consists either in things being as I believed, so that what is believed is indeed what is the case, or in what I correctly believe actually being the reason that I take it to be. Success, then, is not the additional presence of a convenient extra item, but simply the difference between things being as I suppose and not being as I suppose—a difference that is surely inescapable on any account.

Third, the worry that we will find ourselves talking of acting for a reason that is no reason can surely be coped with in other ways. One of these is simply to notice that we are dealing here with an intensional context: the phrase 'acting for a reason' no more requires the user to agree that the reason for which the agent acted was a good reason for so acting than does the phrase 'the grounds on which he acted'. As well as this, one can become more wary of the noun 'reason'. A reason is just a consideration that speaks in favour of action (or belief). Its being the reason it is consists in its so speaking—its supporting this action rather than that one. So a reason that is no reason still exists, in a sense, as the consideration or feature that the agent wrongly took to support acting in the way he proposed, though the supposed reason (or support it gives to acting in the way proposed) does not. In sum, we could hear the remark that he acted for a reason that is no reason as claiming simply that his action can be explained in the standard intentional way, but that the explanation does not reveal anything to be said in favour of what he did.

But these matters are mere skirmishes. The real question is whether any of the argumentation that I gave against theories that the disjunctive conception rejects is also effective against the disjunctive conception itself. And the answer is yes. For in arguing against those who hold that all motivating reasons should be rendered psychologistically, I claimed that to give the agent's reason in the form 'because he believed that p' would, if that were considered to be other than a variant rendition of the simpler 'because p', be to give the wrong explanation. And the second clause of the disjunctive conception—the second disjunct, that is—falls foul of this point too. 'He acted for the reason that p' should not be rendered as 'He acted for the reason that he believed that p', and 'His reason for acting was that p' should not be expressed as 'His reason for acting was that he believed that p' (unless, as always, the suggested re-expressions are intended to be merely variants on their originals). But the second disjunct claims otherwise. So it would be impossible for me, having argued against the fully psychologistic theory, to fall back on the disjunctive conception as an adequate alternative.

One might reply to this point that it depends on our accepting as correct the particular tripartite version that I gave of the disjunctive conception. There is the danger that my tripartite version makes the disjunctive approach weaker than it needs to be, by making it vulnerable to the argumentation given in Chapter 5. Suppose we restrict our attention to what I called the 'less revealing, but still supposedly correct, disjunctive account':

> *A does x for the reason that p* iff
>
> *either* (1) *p* and that *p* is a reason for ϕ-ing and *A* ϕ-s in the light of the fact that *p*
>
> *or* (2) it is for *A* as if (1) were the case.

Here we can see that the second disjunct is not vulnerable to the arguments of Chapter 5. If so, I may have a reason to reject my own tripartite version, but I have no reason to reject the generic form of disjunctivism.

My response to this is that there was something right about my tripartite version, and there is something wrong about the generic form. What is wrong with the latter is the second disjunct. For we don't want to suppose that its seeming to *A* that the first disjunct is the case, i.e. that *p* and that it is a reason for ϕ-ing that *p* and that *A* is ϕ-ing in the light of the fact that *p*, is necessarily a case of *A*'s acting for the reason that *p*. It may only be a case of *A*'s seeming to himself to be acting for the reason that *p*. But, as I have already noted, *A* may be quite mistaken about the reason for which he acted. My tripartite version is not vulnerable to *this* worry, which seems to me to arise on any standard version of disjunctivism. We should accept my tripartite account as the right way to do it—but then, as we have seen, that account should be rejected for a different reason.

2. *Metaphysical Difficulties*

I now turn to consider, or to reconsider, what I take to be the major metaphysical difficulties for the normative account.

The first of these concerns the cases where the agent's belief is false. How can what is believed explain an action when it is not the case? We can understand an action as a response to a feature of the world reasonably well. But what about where the feature is supposed to obtain but does not? Are we not going to be forced to admit that the only thing now capable of explaining the action is the belief—the believing? And once we have admitted this for the case of false belief, won't we have to say the same thing about cases where the belief is true?

One approach here is to look at the same objection in the theory of theoretical reason.[2] Where we adopt the belief that q because of something else that we believe, namely that p, is what we believe only capable of explaining our adopting the belief that q if it is the case that p? Here, I think, we have rather less difficulty in allowing that what is believed, though not the case, explains why we adopted the new belief. (It was required, of course, that we believed those things; but we are catering for this appositionally, perhaps.) And if that is right, it may reveal to us an implicit presupposition that we have been making. One may think of the explanation of action as the attempt to answer the question what can have got this inert body to move. If that is indeed our question, a what-is-believed that is not the case is going to be a very unsatisfying answer; such things just don't seem meaty enough to get a body to move, on any account. It looks as if we are appealing to a nothing to explain a something. But perhaps this way of understanding the question we ask when we look for the explanation of an action can itself be seen as one last expression of Humeanism—something that opposition to Humeanism, or to the psychologism that underlies it, should be very wary of assenting to. Actions, as we know, need not involve bodily movement. Questions of inertia and momentum are not the right ones to raise in discussions of reasons and intentional action. Viewed in this light, it may not seem so improbable that a what-is-believed can explain an action as well as it can a belief, whether what is believed is the case or not.

But such thoughts, though they may help, are surely not enough by themselves to still our doubts. The important point, it seems to me, is that in this area we can have non-factive explanations. There must be some form of words with which we can give the agent's

---

[2] I owe this response to conversations with Peter Hacker.

explanation without committing ourselves to things being as the agent supposed. Whatever one takes that form to be (for instance, 'because, as he supposed, p'), its existence is enough to answer this difficulty. This is because the difficulty is really one about non-factive explanations, rather than, as I originally presented it above, about the ability of non-obtaining states of affairs (or something like that) to make any difference to what happens. It is not that we need a something to get an action going, i.e. start a movement off. The worry is based on the mistaken sense that whatever explains an action must be the case, i.e. that all explanation is factive. We should abandon this and allow that where someone's reason for acting is something that is not the case, that is exactly what it is—something that is not the case. There is no need to look for something else that is the case.

My second difficulty is a more purely metaphysical one. What are these 'things believed' that are supposed to be what explain intentional actions? Are they propositions? Are they states of affairs? Are they facts? In particular, what are they when they are false—if indeed they are capable of falsehood? The issue here is whether to take these questions seriously. If one does take them seriously, the only available answer is regrettably brief. I argued in Chapter 5 that they are not propositions, since they must be things capable of being the case, and no proposition is of that sort. What we believe may be the case or fail to be the case; it may obtain or fail to obtain. Propositions are true or false; they cannot obtain or be the case. But this does not tell us what sort of thing a what-is-believed is when it is not the case—where to place such a 'thing' metaphysically. Perhaps the only answer is that it is something that may or may not be the case. But I do not pretend that this is very enlightening.

The most promising line here is to follow Alan White (1972) in saying that there is no metaphysical problem about the nature of that which is believed when the belief is false, because of the intentionality of belief. A belief can have, as it were, a non-obtaining content without having no content at all. For a non-obtaining content is not the same as a non-existing content. To suppose otherwise is to confuse different sorts of accusatives that go with the verb 'believe'. There is what White calls the 'object-accusative', as in believing the prime minister and believing the rumour that p. If one believes the prime minister, the prime minister must exist; if one believes the rumour that p, that rumour must exist. Then there is the internal accusative 'the belief that p'. This is like 'the suspicion that p', which is what I have when I suspect that p, though it is not what I suspect; no more is the belief that p what I believe when I believe that p, i.e. have the belief that p. However, when one does believe that p, it is certain that one's belief that p exists; in that sense, one cannot have a non-existent belief. Finally there is what White calls the 'intentional-accusative', which is used when we suspect foul play, diagnose measles, doubt someone's sanity, or believe that p. Foul play does not need to exist for us to suspect it, any more than fairies need to exist for us to believe in them, another world war needs to exist for us to fear it, or the trustworthiness of politicians needs to exist for us to rely on it, fools that we are. So intentional-accusatives are not in the business of picking out objects. In that sense, the thing believed (asserted, feared, suspected, diagnosed, reported, relied on) is not an object at all. (Propositions, by contrast, are objects—or they had better be, if they are to be capable of being true.)

My main doubt about this picture concerns whether it allows us to be realist enough about the content of a belief when the belief is true. (If this is right, it is true beliefs rather than false ones that raise difficulties.) If such contents are the sorts of 'thing' that can be the case, what is a content when it is the case? Suppose that the contents of true beliefs are states of affairs, as they need to be if they are to be capable of being good reasons. Does this raise difficulties about the contents of false beliefs? Perhaps all that needs to be said, and all that can be said, is that the content of a belief, what is believed, is something that either is the case or is not.

But this leads to a third difficulty that is hardly metaphysical, but which might be held to undermine my project of trying to show that a motivating reason is capable of being a normative reason. My attempt hinges on the notion of what is believed, which I think of as something that is capable of being the case. Of course not everything that is believed is in fact the case; but everything that is believed must, I have announced, be capable of being so.

What then about beliefs with inconsistent or even just incoherent contents? In such cases there is indeed something that the agent believes; since there is a difference between believing this and believing nothing. But that which is believed is here not capable of being the case. The world could not be the way that agents, in believing these impossibilities, believe it to be. And this appears to break the link between the thing believed and that which is the case.

It is not merely those who want to show a potential coincidence of that which is believed and that which is the case who will have trouble with the contents of incoherent beliefs. Such beliefs have led those who want to understand beliefs in terms of propositions as their contents, and to understand propositions in terms of possible worlds, to talk of impossible possible worlds. We would all prefer to avoid such ontological extravagancies if at all possible. And in the present case I think that we are not driven to them. There is a perfectly acceptable resolution to the problem of impossible belief-contents.

The key to this solution is to notice that that which is believed is *as such* suited to be the case. It is the right sort of thing, as we might say, by contrast with that which is only capable of being true (a proposition or sentence), or of occurring (an event) or existing (a mental state). These other things are the wrong sort of thing to be the case, and this is why they cannot be the case. There are, however, some belief-contents which, although they pass this first test, fail the next. For though *as such* they are the right sort of thing to be the case, they are still incapable of being the case because of the particular content that they are. Examples might be: the contents of false beliefs about the past, the contents of false mathematical beliefs, and the contents of incoherent beliefs of other sorts. There are then two general types of explanation why it is that an object is incapable of being the case. The first is that it is of the wrong metaphysical sort to achieve this feat, so that we explain the matter by showing that *no* event, say, is capable of being the case, and this is an event. The second is that it is of the right sort of thing to achieve this feat, but that it is one of the wrong instances of that sort, so that we explain the matter by showing the nature of the thing that is here believed.

The point, then, is that what is believed always passes the first test, but may still fail the second. That particular instances of things believed may fail the second test causes no damage to my general position. It is the first test that is the important one for my purposes.

An analogy might help. All adults are *as such* entitled to vote. But some adults, because of their own individual qualities, do not have that entitlement (at least in the United Kingdom). They may not have it at all, as where they are very seriously mentally handicapped; or they may have had it and lost it for a while, as where they have been convicted on a criminal charge. By contrast with frogs and stones, all adults are the right sort of thing to have a vote; but some adults do not have the vote, for one reason or another—though always one to do with their own particular nature.

There is a different problem that is of a rather similar type to the one that I have just tried to deal with, which concerns the nature of 'thin' facts such as that the action I have in mind would be wrong. This is, let us say, what I believe, and it is in fact the case. The consideration in the light of which I hold back is that it would be wrong to act in this way. But that this is so cannot be among the reasons against the action. That fact—or state of affairs, I should say— cannot be among the reasons against doing the action. For it itself obtains for various reasons, and *these* are the reasons why the act is wrong, and they make up *all* the reasons against doing it that are either necessary or possible. That the action is wrong cannot, therefore, be among the reasons against doing it; similarly, that the action we propose would in fact be right cannot be among the reasons in favour of doing it. It follows from these considerations that we have here something that motivates, or at least something capable of being a motivating reason, that is not capable of being a good reason. Is this a problem for my account? I want to say that it is not.

The crucial question for me has all along been whether something is the *right sort of thing* to be a reason of a certain sort. These thin motivators are indeed the right sort of thing to be good reasons, being states of affairs. That they cannot actually achieve the status for which they are metaphysically equipped is explained by appeal to their special type of content. The situation is therefore rather like the one I was describing in response to the previous difficulty: the metaphysical requirements have been met, and that is all that is required for my account, even though it is correct to say that we here have something capable of motivating as a reason and not capable of being a good reason. What might have made it seem that there was a difficulty here was merely the constant rhetoric of this book, in which I speak consistently of acting for the reason that p, where the reason in favour of acting is also that p.

3. *Internalism and Desire-Based Reasons Again*

The next three sections return us to the concerns of Chapter 2. I offered there a supposedly conclusive argument against the desire-based reasons thesis (the DBR thesis). But that argument may still have seemed to amount to little more than a reassertion of the true but question-begging claim that if we have no reason to adopt the end, our adoption of the end can give us no reason to do what will subserve that end. For those who suspect that this is so, I now offer a different argument against desire-based reasons. This further argument appeals to the normative story, that is, to the account of motivation developed in Chapters 5 and 6. It is, however, also available to the pure cognitivist, and I will be expressing it in terms that are designed to reveal that fact.

The normative story holds that our reasons for action—the ones that motivate us, the things that explain both motivation and action—are things we believe rather than our believing those things. But it accepts the move that lies at the bottom of pure cognitivism, the identification of desiring with being motivated. So, like pure cognitivism, it insists that the explanation of desire must always be given in cognitive terms. It only differs from then on. On either account, then, desire is not (any part of) what motivates. If this is so, it would be odd, to say the least, if all our normative reasons stemmed somehow from our desires. The oddity at issue lies in the suggestion that this would deprive those reasons of the ability to influence our actions. For if our desires are not what motivate us, it cannot be that our reasons motivate us, if reasons are grounded in our desires. If reasons were grounded in desires, that would be an account of how it is that desires motivate us, which we have already rejected as a possibility.

The oddity I am trying to bring out here lies in the suggestion that my wanting something should be able to give me a (normative) reason to act in a certain way, but not to be capable of influencing my action as an element in what motivates. This is how things would be if we accepted the normative approach to motivation (or indeed pure cognitivism, if it comes to that), while holding that all our reasons are grounded in our desires.

One might worry that this argument is effectively circular. In terms of the overall structure of this book, I argued against desire-based reasons in Chapter 2, and then used the objectivity of normative reasons that was thus established to argue against psychologism in the theory of motivation in Chapter 5. Now, it might seem, I am trying to use my anti-psychologistic approach to motivation as the basis for a further argument against desire-based reasons. Things are not really so, however, as we can see when we remember that this further argument is effectively also available to the pure cognitivist (as I tried to show in the way I expressed it above). I could have given this argument in Chapter 4, in terms of pure cognitivism; and this would have shown that the basis of the argument is really the cognitivism that is common to the pure theory of Chapter 4 and the normative story of Chapter 5. But if I had done so, it would have been apparently undermined by the way in which I abandon all forms of psychologism immediately afterwards.

I think of the argument as a triangulation argument, since it appeals to results in the theory of motivation to establish results in the theory of (good) reasons. If it is sound, can a similar one be used to refute internalism? Can we now show not only that actual desires of the agent are not necessary as grounds for any practical reason that the agent may have, but also that potential desires are not necessary conditions for the agent's reasons to be the reasons that they are? There is just a chance that our triangulation argument against the DBR thesis will also succeed in unsettling internalism, despite the differences between these two targets. We are considering the suggestion that there needs to be a potential desire in the agent for the agent to have any reason to act, though no actual desire can play a role in motivating the agent. Any reason that the agent already has must be capable of motivating him, of course, since, as internalism sees things, the agent would not have such a reason if he would not be motivated accordingly, that is, have the appropriate desires, in condition C. So there are two possibilities. The first is that the agent already has a relevant desire which he would retain in condition C, but that this desire is not to be thought of as part of what would there motivate the agent (because we have adopted cognitivism, in one form or another). The second is that the agent does not yet have a relevant desire, but would have one in appropriate circumstances, i.e. condition *C*, and that when he does come to have the desire, it will be similarly prevented from contributing in any way to what motivates him. Could one say that both of these scenarios are incoherent? The idea would have to be that once the desire has been got in there, it is too late to prevent it from contributing to motivation, in just the sort of way we have rejected. But this does not seem to be a correct picture of the situation. Let us remind ourselves of our present formulation of internalism (from Chapter 2.1):

> That it is the case that *p* is a good reason for *A* to *φ only if* there is some *e* such that in condition *C A* would desire *e* and, given that *p*, *φ*-ing subserves the prospect of *e*'s being realized (or continuing to be realized).

We could replace 'desire' in this formulation by an explicit allusion to motivation, thus:

> That it is the case that *p* is a good reason for *A* to *φ only if* there is some *e* such that in condition *C A* would be motivated by the prospect of *e*'s being realized (or continuing to be realized), and, given that *p*, *φ*-ing would subserve that prospect.

And it is clear in this formulation that there is no suggestion that *A* is motivated by anything other than the prospect of its becoming or remaining the case that *e*, which is entirely consistent with the demands of the normative story.[3] So this triangulation argument fails to unsettle internalism. For the moment, then, I put the project of refuting internalism aside; it will return in the next section.

Against the DBR thesis, however, the triangulation argument seems to be successful. Its premises are of course hotly contested, but given those premises the DBR thesis fails. Perhaps it is not surprising that a purely cognitive theory of motivation should be at odds with a desire-based account of reasons, once we allow that any good reason should be capable of motivating the agent for whom it is a reason. But even though the fact itself is not surprising, it is surprisingly hard to establish it.

---

[3] Note that the formulation is also consistent with the demands of pure cognitivism if we understand a prospect as a belief.

4. *Defusing Internalism*

We have found no route to a direct refutation of Williams' internalism. But in this section I consider the philosophical motivations that underlie that position, and try to show how those motivations can, at least to some extent, be met or assimilated by adherents of the normative story. Though Williams expresses his position in a way that is informed by Humeanism throughout, it seems to me that when re-expressed in the terms we have come to favour, much of the pressure he applies can be absorbed and, to a degree, neutralized.

First, there is the question how it is that a reason can be a reason for an agent if it does not in some way key into his present motivational structure. This question is one that, if it has force, can still have force for us. What makes the question appear at odds with our approach is an implicit identification of 'motivational structure' as the agent's '*S*', understood as a pattern of motivating desires. If we understand the agent's present motivational structure in terms of the considerations that motivate him,[4] there is no temptation to suppose that the agent must already have or be able to get relevant motivating desires if he is to have any reasons. As we saw in the previous section, we could say instead that the agent must already be motivated by some relevant good, or be capable of being got to be motivated by such a good starting from where he now is, if the prospect of that good is to be able now to give him a reason to act one way rather than another. This would tie the agent's reasons to the agent's present motivation in a way that does nothing to sustain Williams' focus on desires as motivators. But of course we could also understand 'motivational structure' as a structure of motivatednesses, that is, as we now see it, as a structure of desires conceived of as states of being motivated.

What this shows, I think, is that it is pointless to try to refute internalism merely on the basis of this or that theory of motivation—whether it be the normative story or pure cognitivism. The internalist constraint on normative reasons can be re-expressed in terms of whatever approach to motivation one prefers. On the other hand, we have also been shown that the pressure in favour

---

[4] Or in terms of the beliefs that motivate him, as the pure cognitivist would have it.

of internalism does not come from any thoughts about the basic role played by desire, or anything like that, but from two further questions.

The first of these asks how a consideration can be a reason for an agent to act if it does not relate in some special way to *him*. Suppose we were to say, as the normative story has it, that it is not so much that the agent believes such and such that gives him a reason to act, but what he believes, e.g. that this is a bomb. That this is a bomb does not itself especially relate to this agent; it is just a state of affairs. But we surely want to say that no considerations are 'reasons in themselves'—there are no reasons hanging around out there, waiting to find someone to be for or to belong to. To be a reason is to be a reason for a particular person, and to do that, the reason has to latch onto that person in a special way.

The reply to this might be that there are several ways in which this might be achieved, and plenty of them are still available to us. For instance, we might suppose that a consideration only serves to create a reason for an agent if that agent has a relevant opportunity for action. The reason to act only arises for those agents who have some opportunity to act. There may be some people in need in Peru but whom I have no reason to help, having no opportunity to do so. As soon as I get the opportunity, their need begins to give me a reason to act in one way rather than in another.

So far so good. But there is a particular version of the question we are currently considering that is not so easily dealt with. This concerns bluff. One of Williams' reasonable aims is to rule out certain forms of bluff. The one that surfaces in his initial article (1980) involves the attempt by Owen Wingrave's father to persuade Owen that the family's fairly glorious military tradition is a reason for Owen to take up a career in the army. Owen has no interests that could possibly be subserved by such a life. Williams thinks of Owen's father's remarks as bluff or bluster, and wants to provide a sort of formal hurdle that they will fail to clear, and by so failing reveal that there is no reason *for Owen* here.

An externalist should, I think, be sympathetic to this. But this sympathy should be linked with a robust sense that it is possible for there to be a good available for someone that they are not yet motivated by and that purely rational means would be unable to get them to be motivated by, starting from where they now are. The problem, then, is how to sustain Williams' antipathy towards bluff or bluster, without ruling out external reasons.

If one wishes to do this, there is perhaps an available method. This is to distinguish between thoughts about what is a good and thoughts about what is a good for a particular person. This distinction is different from that between what is good and that which a particular person does, or would, in condition *C*, recognize as good. We could do something against bluff and bluster by demanding that all reasons for an individual are grounded in value for that individual—in something that is of value for him as he is presently constituted, or more probably would be of value for him if he were in condition *C*. There might be no purely rational way of getting him into a situation in which a military career, or the continuation of the family military tradition, would be of value for him. In this case, the suggestion that he has a reason to enter the army is just bluff. But it is also possible that in condition *C* there would be something of value for Owen in the military life, though he would not recognize this value. And this possibility is sufficient to ensure that the reasons grounded in that value are external reasons.

Much would need to be done, of course, to build up this distinction between what is of value and what is of value for an agent. In particular, if we want to defend the possibility of moral reasons as usually conceived, we would need either to show that moral value is of value for all agents whatever, or to draw a distinction here between moral reasons and other reasons in such a way that we can defensibly say that moral reasons are not subject to the revised internalist constraint. The former route looks more promising, I think.

The main point, though, is that one does not need to introduce a constraint based upon the individual's ability to be got to be motivated by a reason for that reason to exist. And it was that sort of constraint that we were trying to avoid, in the name of a certain 'objective' approach to reasons.

The third form of pressure in favour of internalist constraints on reasons derives from Williams' claim (1980: 109) that every reason for a given agent must be capable of motivating that agent, and that, as soon as it does so, it becomes an internal reason. The answer to this is more trenchant (see Parfit 1997: 114–16). A reason that is external in Williams's sense is capable of motivating, and of remaining external while doing so. We can, that is, be motivated by a con-

sideration which would have given us a reason even if we neither
had been motivated by it, nor would have been so motivated even
if we had known more and thought more clearly. The fact that we
are motivated by it does not show that its normative status as a
reason for us depends on our being actually or potentially motivated by it. So a reason can remain external, in the relevant sense,
even while actually motivating.

In these ways I hope to absorb the pressure that Williams is apply-
ing without being forced to move away from the normative story.

5. *Degrees of Objectivity*

My main purpose in Chapters 2 and 3 was to refute the claim that
our reasons are grounded in or given us by contingencies of our
own psychological make-up. There were two main ways in which
this could have been true. Our having a reason to ϕ could be made
the case by our having certain desires, or by our having certain
beliefs. But in each case I argued that our reasons are given us by
features of the situation, rather than by our own psychological
states—unless those states function merely as features of the
situation. Our reasons, as I have put it on occasions, are objective
rather than subjective or relative to our psychology.

In order to establish this position, there has been no need to
refute internalism. The internalist, I have been allowing, can
happily allow most views about which sort of features are the
ground of our reasons. For internalists are only interested in imposing a certain constraint on reasons, not in pronouncing on grounds.

None the less, I would really prefer, if possible, to establish a
greater degree of objectivity for normative reasons than that which
I have got so far. Here are four 'subjectivist' claims:

1. Reasons are grounded in subjective contingencies of the
   agent;
2. That which is desired only gives us a reason on condition that
   we desire it;
3. That which we believe only gives us a reason on condition that
   we believe it;
4. Reasons are dependent on their ability to be recognized and
   accepted as such by the agent.

In Chapters 2 and 3 I argued against the first three of these. But the fourth remained. It is distinct from the two before it, because it speaks of accepting and recognizing *as a reason* or *as reason-giving*, rather than (as the second and third claim do) of accepting and recognizing that which gives the reason. And if internalism were true, the fourth subjectivist claim would be true. For if it is a necessary condition on each of agent A's reasons that A would be motivated by that reason in condition C, this is a sense in which reasons for A are dependent on their acceptance and recognition by A. Those reasons may exist without A's recognizing them as reasons, even if internalism is true. But their existence requires that A would be motivated accordingly in condition C. And this is enough to make the fourth subjectivist claim true. That is why I am still trying to find a way of undermining the demands of internalism.

8

How Many Explanations?

1. *Explanation and Causal Explanation*

In this book I have argued against certain prevalent views about motivating reasons, the reasons for which we act. Such reasons are the things we appeal to when we try to explain (or at least to explain in a certain way) why someone did what he did. So a theory of such reasons contains, or is, a theory about the nature of a certain sort of explanation of action—and vice versa. As readers may have noticed, however, I have tried to discuss this issue without making much use, if any, of the distinction between the causal and the non-causal. I have avoided asking whether this or that form of explanation is causal, and I have avoided asking whether the things we specify as the reasons why someone acted are to be thought of as causes of his so acting. But this question, or rather these questions, can no longer be shirked. I start with the question whether explanation by appeal to the agent's reasons, which we might call normative explanation, is itself causal.

Many people think of causation as an objective relation between particular events, a relation that constitutes 'the cement of the universe'. The prospects for thinking of motivating reasons, as they are understood by the normative story, in such terms seem rather remote. Even if we do want to understand as causal the 'because' that we often use to link the action to the reasons for which it was done, we would need to be thinking in terms of 'fact-causation' rather than 'event-causation'.[1] One might decide not to do an action for the reason that it would be wrong; but that it would be wrong is hardly an event; it looks much more like a fact. Now there are three views about our talk of one fact causing another, or of a

---

[1] For the distinction between fact-causation and event-causation, see Vendler (1962) and more generally Mellor (1995) and Steward (1997).

fact causing an event (as we might say, the fact that his wife was going to leave him caused him to take his own life). The first understands it either as a different way of expressing a causal relation holding between events, or merely as a form of explanation and so quite different from the objective relation between particulars that obtains when one event causes another. On either version of this view, there is only one causal relation, and that is event-causation (Davidson 1980, ch. 7; Hornsby 1995). This view would probably take the 'because' that links actions and the reasons for which they are done to be not so much a causal one as a 'causal-explanatory' one.

The second view takes fact-causation to consist, not in a merely explanatory relation, but in a distinct objective relation that holds between facts rather than between particulars such as events or objects (Steward 1997, ch. 6). The idea here is that as well as the relation of 'making happen' that combines cause and effect when both are events, there is a second relation of 'making the case' which is (or one form of which is) causal. What made them unable to persuade the jury was that their main argument was so obviously flawed, perhaps. Steward understands this sort of causal relation as a intensional relation of causal relevance, quite different from the extensional relation that holds between events. But both relations are worth thinking of as causal, despite their differences, because both are to do with what we need to do to ensure or prevent things from happening (events) or from being the case (facts).

The third view denies the existence of event-causation altogether and makes do with relations between facts (Mellor 1995). On this view, all apparently event-causal statements can be converted without loss, and indeed with gain, into fact-causal statements. Instead of saying that the lighting of the match (event) caused the fire (event), we say that what made it the case that a fire began (fact) was that the match was struck (fact), just as we might say that what made it the case that a fire did not begin (fact) was that the match was wet (fact). Unlike Steward, however, Mellor tends to see these fact-causal statements as explanations rather than expressions of a distinct objective relation obtaining between facts.

Let us suppose for the moment that the second view is correct, in our most liberal spirit. As well as the causal relation between particular events, we now allow a quite distinct but still causal and objective relation that holds between facts. This picture allows the normal understanding of the supposedly event-causal relation between psychological states and action, but is also hospitable to the way in which the normative story understands acting (or refraining) for a reason, since that the action would be wrong is a much better candidate for the title of 'fact' than it was for that of 'event'. Still, are we happy to think that moral and other normative facts can stand in that objective relation to facts about bodily movements (or even directly to bodily movements conceived as particulars, since devotees of fact-causation often claim that a fact can explain an event)? Can a body be caused to move by the fact that one person owes another a favour?

This sort of metaphysically based doubt about whether normative explanation can be causal is not much more than a suspicion. There is a further consideration, however, to be added to it, which is decisive. For if normative explanation is non-factive, as argued in Chapter 6, it surely cannot be associated with any relation worth calling causal. So we have sufficient reason to suppose that the relation between reasons and action is not causal, and we have sufficient reason to suppose that the explanation of action by appeal to reasons—normative explanation, as we are calling it—is not causal either.

This might seem to be a telling blow against the normative story. For don't we know by now that action-explanation is in the business of specifying (or at least alluding to) causes of the action explained? What about Davidson's master argument[2] that the reasons for which the action was done *must* be (among) its causes? Though expressed in terms of Davidson's view that what others might call fact-causation is more a form of explanation than a different sort of causal relation, Davidson's argument can actually be used by devotees of fact-causation equally well. The argument is that we might have available more than one belief capable of explaining our action, as Davidson would put it, or, in our terms, more than one reason to do it. We might have done it either to please Sue or to annoy her husband. In such a situation, what makes it the case that one of these is the reason

---

[2] This argument occurs in very abbreviated form in his 'Actions, Reasons, Causes', repr. in Davidson (1980: 3–19, at p. 9; cf. also p. 11).

for which we act rather than the other? Davidson's answer to this question is an appeal to causation: one caused the action and the other did not. Can non-causal accounts (whether of action-explanation or of the relation between reasons and action) do as well?[3]

It is not obvious to me that causal approaches do really have the advantage here that Davidson supposes. His idea is that to characterize the relation between reason and action as causal is to make a move beyond saying that these features were one's reason for action and those were not. I think that we need to distinguish two thoughts here. The first is the idea that there is a philosophical theory of causation to give theoretical depth to the distinction in terms of causes, while there is no equivalent theory of support by reasons to give philosophical depth to the non-causal alternative. A different way of putting this point is to say that the causal approach sees the relation between reasons and actions as philosophically analysable, while the non-causal one does not. The second thought is that the causal approach does not see the truth that these things were my reasons and those were not as a *bare* truth; for causalists, this truth holds in virtue of another truth, while for non-causalists it does not. The two contrasts are different, because a bare truth might still be analysable. But both contrasts seem to me to be dubious.

---

[3] There is a complication here derived from the fact that Davidson thinks that where there is an instance of the causal relation, there must be a law, but that there are no laws linking psychological states and actions. There are laws linking physical events and bodily movements, however (and all actions are bodily movements), and all psychological states are physical (probably neural) occurrences of some sort. But because laws are linguistic objects, they are sensitive to the terms in which they are phrased; they must be phrased in physical terms. So it appears that for the purposes of explanation of action, we need to talk in psychological terms, but that the underlying causal reality is physical. Things are held together by the identity of psychological state and physical state, but the psychological explanation is not the same explanation as the physical one. (See Davidson 1980, chs. 11–13.)

How then are we to understand the master argument? The point has to be that, of all the truths capable of explaining the action, only one *really* explains it. That truth picks out a psychological state which is a physical state that stood in the real causal relation to the bodily movement that is the action. But the sort of rational relation that stands between the agent's beliefs and his acting in the way he did, though vital to the ordinary explanation of the action, has in fact nothing to do with the causal explanation of why those particular bodily movements took place. The explanation of the movements is physical, and that of the action is psychological, but the psychological state referred to in the second explanation is identical with the physical state referred to in the former one.

As far as the first goes, the appeal to the existence of a philo-sophical theory of causation is only effective in the present context if that theory is actually able to distinguish an active from an inac-tive but potential cause, and it is well known that many theories of causation are incapable of drawing that distinction. (Take the problem of overdetermination for counterfactual analyses of cau-sation as a notorious case.) In fact, I don't know of one that I do think capable of this feat.

The second contrast, in terms of bareness, is not itself very effec-tive; if causal truths were bare truths, the fact that the causal approach gives us a move before we reach bareness is not, I think, a great theoretical advantage. It is no help here to say that a causal story can always be unpacked, or broken down into micro-elements. For, first, it is not clear that this is true in the present case; second, it might be that the notion of causation is itself bare at every stage of the unpacking. I think that the contrast in terms of bareness really requires the other contrast, in terms of theoretical depth. But, as I have said, I think the latter contrast would only be effective if the theory of causation were in better shape than it is at present.

The most direct response to Davidson, however, is just to say that the difference between those reasons for which the agent did in fact act and those for which he might have acted but did not is not a difference in causal role at all. It is just the dif-ference between the considerations in the light of which he acted and other considerations which he took to favour acting as he did but which were not in fact the ones in the light of which he decided to do it. This is admittedly not very informa-tive, since we have to allow that we have offered no analysis or philosophical account of the 'in the light of' relation. I suspect, however, that no such analysis or account is available to be given, without therefore supposing that this has any tendency to show that the relation concerned does not exist. It is what it is, and not another thing; and if it cannot be analysed, so much the worse for the more global pretensions of analysis. (I agree, however, that it would be good to produce an *account* of the 'in the light of' relation—if one could only think of some way of producing one.)

I conclude that normative explanation of action neither is nor needs to be causal.

2. *Combining the Causal and the Normative*

The issue to which I now turn is the relation between our normative, non-causal explanations on the one side and putatively causal
explanations on the other. Is it possible for there to be both styles
of explanation running in tandem, so that even if my attempt to
defend the normative story were deemed successful, one might still
try to defend a non-normative, causal form of explanation of action
as well? Could there be, that is, two distinct, equipollent, and non-
competing forms of action-explanation available at once? In terms
of the forms of explanation that I have considered in Chapters 5
and 6, this question amounts to asking whether we could not add
to normative explanation either event-causal explanations in terms
of psychological states or fact-causal explanations which offer as
the cause of an action the fact that the agent believed as he did.

The idea of there being two equally good forms of explanation
in this area is very attractive, since it offers the prospect of a philosophical compromise, always the last refuge of the feeble-minded.
And in general I have no objection to one and the same thing being
doubly explained; I do not suppose that we can rule out this possibility in advance. Arthur Collins argues (Collins 1984) that teleological and causal explanations are compatible in biology—and
even that without the support of causal explanations, teleological
ones would appear miraculous and have to be abandoned. His
example is that of homeostasis. A homeostatic system operates in
such a way as to maintain a certain equilibrium. We explain the
operations of the system teleologically, by appeal to their effects.
But we know that, if such an explanation is to be possible, there
must be some way in which the system works; for otherwise the
whole thing would be a miracle. There has to be a causal explanation, that is, to run in tandem with the teleological one. And the
same is true in reverse; the causal explanation, though complete of
its sort, needs the teleological explanation to support it, for otherwise we will be unable to answer the question why 'just the right
change needed to cause *this* effect will be the one that occurs'
(Collins 1987: 126).

I do not mean to suggest that Collins is clearly right about all
this. In particular, there are other views about the relation between
supposedly teleological and causal explanations in biology; one of
these is that teleological explanations are abridged versions of

causal explanations in terms of natural selection (Wright 1976). My point is rather that it would not be very persuasive to argue merely that since actions can be explained normatively, they cannot *also* be explained causally. It is better to allow that there can be two concurrent explanations of the same event, of quite different styles. The homeostasis example stands merely as a supposed instance of such a thing. It is, however, one whose structural aspects I find interesting, and I shall make occasional appeal to them in what follows.

Further, if we allow that causal explanation is factive and explanation by appeal to reasons non-factive, we might reasonably conclude that the two forms of explanation *cannot* conflict. For whatever logical space is occupied by the one can surely not be identical with that offered by the other. The relation between them will be more like that between Davidson's extensional and intensional causal statements (Davidson 1980, ch. 7, esp. 161–2). This does not mean that the intensional–extensional distinction is the same as the factive–non-factive one. Davidson's causal explanations are intensional because substitution of one true description of an object by another in them may change the truth value of the whole.[4] But for a causal explanation to be true, as Davidson conceives the matter, the contained sentences must be true; so all such explanations are factive.[5] I only mean that just as Davidson's causal explanations can hardly conflict with true causal statements, so it is difficult to see in advance how my non-factive ones could conflict with ordinary factive ones, of either type.

This may be so. But the argument of this book has, sadly, not been so conciliatory. For in attempting to build up the prospects for the normative story, I found myself arguing against, not all forms of

---

[4] As may substitution of one extensionally equivalent sentence for another—but I am not sure that this is really the point. See n. 5 below.

[5] It is common to suppose that intensionality (understood as description-sensitivity) and non-factiveness go together. (Part of the explanation of this view is the influence of Frege's contention that truth values are the referents of sentences, though this may be to put the cart before the horse.) But they don't go together. Subjunctive conditionals, I think, are extensional but non-factive (where not explanatory). Causal explanation, as Davidson supposes, is factive but intensional; the explanation of action, as I understand it, is intensional and non-factive. Contexts that are both extensional and factive are the norm. It is worth noting that the anti-causalist tradition in the debate about the explanation of action has tended to stress the intensional nature of action-explanation, when in my view it should be stressing its non-factiveness (e.g. Stoutland 1976).

potentially causal explanation of action, but the two forms that we currently have in mind, namely psychologism and the 'new theory'. As before, I take psychologism first here. Consider the claims of Parfit (1997: 114n.):

motivating reasons can be acceptably regarded in two ways. On the *psychological account*, motivating reasons are beliefs and/or desires, when these explain our decisions and our acts. On the *non-psychological account*, motivating reasons are *what* we believe and/or *what* we want. Thus, when asked, 'Why did he jump?', we might truly claim: 'Because the hotel was on fire', or 'Because he believed the hotel was on fire', or 'To save his life', or 'Because he wanted to save his life'.

Since both accounts are acceptable, we should accept both, and should thus conclude that there are two kinds of motivating reason: one kind are mental states, the other are the contents or objects of these states. These two kinds of reason always go together. For some purposes, especially normative discussion, the non-psychological account is more natural; for others, such as causal explanation, we must appeal to the psychological account.

I suggest that it is best to understand Parfit here as claiming not that there are two kinds of motivating reason, but just that there are two forms that the explanation of action can take, and that wherever we find a true explanation of one form, we can construct from it a true explanation of the other form. In this sense, the two forms of explanation 'always go together'.

Now it may seem that this position admits the view that I am arguing for, since it allows that there is a form of explanation of action that is exactly as the normative story has it. All that Parfit is saying is that the coherence of this story is not challenged by allowing also that we can explain action by appeal to psychological states of the agent. The implication is that defenders of the normative story should be satisfied by his admission that their account makes good philosophical sense—something that has often been denied. They should not seek further to undermine the coherence of psychologism. This, however, seems to me to distort the strategical situation in two ways. The first is that it is not agreed on all sides that explanations of the form 'He did it because he believed that *p*' or 'His reason for doing it was that he believed that *p*' achieve explanation by specifying a psychological state of the agent. I tried to suggest in Chapter 6 that there is another way of seeing things on this point, by distinguishing between psychologism in its various forms and what I called 'the new theory'. The second distortion is that it is not as if no arguments have been offered directly against the coherence of psychologism. In Chapter 5 I argued that the psychologistic story fails to meet at least one of the two main constraints on accounts of motivating reasons. Either it fails to show how it is possible for the reason in the light of which we acted to have been among the reasons in favour of acting, or it fails to show how it is possible more generally for a motivating reason to be a good reason for action and so renders us incapable of acting for a good reason. If those arguments are sound, they are as sound against the view that psychologism is the only truth as they are against the view that psychologism is true but not the only truth.

It is therefore impossible for me to be very welcoming to the suggestion that psychologistic explanation of action, understood as an alternative form of explanation in terms of the reasons for which the action was done, is perfectly all right in its own way. If causal explanations of action are to be possible, I must say, at least they cannot include psychologistic ones except in other than a reason-specifying style. (If clinical psychologists come up with causal explanations of action in terms of psychological states that do not pretend to capture the reasons agents have and for which they act, that is of course a different matter.)

Even if my argument for the coherence of the normative story had not been partly based on supposed inadequacies of psychologistic explanations, it is worth asking whether we should think of the present case, in which we are supposing that we might run psychologistic and normative explanations in tandem, as an appropriate example of the admitted possibility that there should be two forms of explanation of the same event at once. But the models we have for that possibility differ in significant ways from the present case. Consider Collins's model of causal and teleological explanations of the operation of a valve. There was one explanation of the opening of the valve in terms of what it would achieve (the stabilization of temperature) and another in terms of how it worked (the nature of the mechanism and how it responded to certain triggers). The salient features of these two explanations are quite different. In particular, and most obviously, the teleological explanation appeals to what is to happen and the causal explanation appeals to what has happened. This being so, the chances of their conflicting

are surely much reduced. And we are encouraged in this by noticing that there is a sense in which the two explanations direct
themselves towards different aspects of the situation. The causal
explanation tells us how it works, and the teleological explanation
tells us what it is for.

When we turn to the supposed compatibility, and, one hopes,
even mutual support, of the psychologistic and normative explanation, we find neither of these features. First, all the features that
are in play in the one are also in play in the other. We have the psychological state, the believing, on the one side, and the thing
believed, the thing that is supposedly the case, on the other. The
two explanations differ from each other in the ways in which they
conceive the interrelations between these two features. One sees
the operative feature as the psychological state, ascribing a subor-
dinate role to the thing believed. The other sees things quite the
opposite way round. It is, I suggest, odd to suppose that both can
be right.

The second point is more telling. For the two forms of explanation directly contradict each other on the nature of the reasons that
motivate us. Asked what motivates us, one explanation says that we
are motivated by our own psychological states and the other says
that we are not. How can they both be right?

Third, it is hard to distinguish between the questions answered
by the two explanations in the way that we did for the example of
homeostasis. That example was offered as one in which we might
have something worth thinking of as two mutually supporting
explanations of one and the same thing, namely the opening of a
valve, and the two explanations direct themselves towards one and
the same question (namely, Why did this happen?), even though
there is a sense in which they take that question differently, as
'What is it for?' and as 'What led to this?' The competing pretensions of the normative and the psychologistic explanations of
action are not so easily reconciled. For they both seem to be trying
to answer both questions at once.

One might attempt a final defence of psychologism at this point,
taking it as a merely causal theory in the spirit of Chapter 1.2, and
abandoning all normative pretensions entirely. This would make
my earlier arguments against it irrelevant, since those arguments
amounted to saying that psychologism cannot succeed in showing
that the 'reasons' for which we act are capable of being good ones.

39

If the theory defends itself by drawing in its horns and ceasing altogether to talk of reasons, it is immune to such attacks.

The question remains, however, whether this 'merely causal' version of psychologism is itself coherent. The theory has now ceased to be a theory about motivating reasons, and thereby, I would have thought, ceased to be a theory of motivation. But if it is not a theory of motivation, it is not clear what the question is to which it is attempting to give a causal answer. The agent's beliefs, now, are causes of his actions, but they in no way represent the light in which he acted, or chose to do what he did. This seems incoherent to me. The only way that those beliefs could act as causes is by being the light in which the agent acted, and if that is what they are doing, they are back in the business of reasons-explanation whether they like it or not. In sum, the 'merely causal' version of psychologism seems to be an unstable halfway house between genuine causal explanation, on one side, and genuine reasons-explanation on the other.

I do not mean by this to deny that people often have beliefs that influence their actions but do not do so by virtue of being taken as reasons. Apparently those who believe that steps are already being taken to remedy the situation are more likely to give to charitable causes. We need not take this to mean that this consideration is among the features in the light of which they choose to make their donations. It might only mean that the belief predisposes them to give, while their giving is done for other reasons. This could still be a causal matter, without incoherence. The critical remarks of the previous paragraph were directed towards the more general claim that *every* reasons-explanation could be attended with a merely causal psychologistic explanation in which the very same beliefs are now acting as causes.

None of this does anything to show that the beliefs and desires of the agent, conceived as psychological states, are utterly irrelevant to the explanation of action. We have already allotted to them a perfectly good place, as enabling conditions within an explanation of the now familiar normative style.

Psychologism is, however, not the only form of potentially causal theory. In Chapter 6.1 I drew a distinction between two ways of understanding 'He did it because he believed that p'. The first, psychologism, is run in terms of event-causation, seeing his action as an event caused by a psychological state which is, if not exactly an event, still at least event-like. Second was what I called 'the new theory', which really tried to understand 'He did it because he believed that *p*' as specifying a relation between his action and the state of affairs of his believing that *p*, which we could for present purposes think of as a fact. Thinking now in terms of this new theory, could we not suppose that it appeals to a potentially causal relation between his action and the fact that he believed that *p*, one which is compatible with the normative relation between his action and the good reason for doing it, namely the fact that *p*?

Not, I think, if we accept the arguments given in Chapter 6. The main argument of 6.1 was that thinking of motivating reasons always as 'that he believes that *p*' in preference to the simpler 'that *p*' gives the wrong account of most of the reasons why we act. If that is right, we make no improvement in moving from the event-causal picture of psychologism to the fact-causal picture of the new theory. Since the new theory gives the wrong account of the reasons why we act, it matters nothing whether that account is or is not somehow compatible with the right account.

This may seem too quick. Consider, then, the position pro-pounded by Ingmar Persson, which is that there are normally two explanations of an action, one that lays out the light in which the agent made the decision he did, and the other psychological. Persson's views exemplify perfectly the combination whose pos-sibility we are currently considering, because for him the psycho-logical explanation is not conceived as specifying psychological *states* of the agent, but rather psychological *facts* such as 'that he believed that *p*'. He writes (in a private communication), 'On my account, the agent's reason for doing *x* may be that doing *x* would bring it about that *p* (make him rich, save someone's life), whereas the reason why he did *x* would then be (the fact) that he believes that doing *x* would bring it about that *p*.' So as Persson sees it, there are two concurrent explanations of the action. One gives the agent's reason, and the other gives the reason why he did it. The former is non-factive and non-causal, the latter factive and causal.

As I have already said, there is no general ban on one and the same thing's having two explanations of different styles. My reason for rejecting the picture that Persson offers us derives from special features of the case before us. He so carves things up that the agent's reason for doing what he did can never be among the reasons why he acted; indeed, it is the wrong *sort of thing* to be the reason why (or for which?) he acted, and I think of this as simply paradoxical. If we said to the agent 'You can tell us as often as you like what your reason was for doing what you did, but we know in advance that that reason can never be the reason why you did it', I think he would feel rightly insulted—and this even though we are not disputing the *truth* of what he tells us.

A further stumbling-block lies in the fact that in the case where everything is going well (there being no mistake or confusion on the agent's part, for instance), the explanation of the action that specifies the considerations in the light of which the agent acted seems, as it were, to be complete, so that there is nothing for the second explanation to do. This would mean that there are somehow *too many* explanations around. What is disconcerting about the situation as conceived by Persson is that the two explanations seem to run over the same material, and it is hard to see how the very same material could be the ground for two quite different explanations, both 'correct' in their own terms, of the agent acting as he did. This situation is quite different from the one that Collins discusses; causal and teleological explanations of homeostasis appeal to quite different considerations.

3. *Further Causal Explanations*

I am now supposing that causal explanations of action that appeal to psychological states of the agent as causes, as well as those that appeal to the fact that the agent is in those states, are ruled out either by what has gone before, or because the place they are trying to occupy has been given to something else better suited to the job. But there remain other forms of causal explanation of action whose ability to combine with normative explanation remains to be considered.[6]

The first of these is neural explanation. We can think of this as a 'how it works' explanation, rather like the explanation of how the valve was got to open. As such, it bids fair not to compete with the normative explanation, which plays effectively the role of the

---

[6] Jennifer Hornsby asks this question, in a way, in Hornsby (1995). But since she accepts a psychologistic understanding of reason-based explanation of action, her suggestions about the supposed compatibility of explanations of action in terms of reasons and neural explanations of movements are of no help to me.

teleological one in the homeostasis model. Now there is no point in denying either the availability or the relevance of neural accounts of what is going on. At least, this is so for all actions that involve some bodily movement. If the body does move itself, there will surely be some story to be told at the neurological level about how this movement came to happen. If all actions involved bodily movement, there would be such a story to be told for all actions whatever. Sadly for the lovers of the simple, however, there are actions for which no movement is required at all, such as that of reciting a favourite poem to oneself. The attractions of a 'how it works' explanation are not so obvious in these cases as in the case of the raising of an arm. It is not obvious that there needs to be such a thing at all. That is, it is not obvious that there needs to be a story relating the silent poetry recital to the neural in the sort of way that the raising of an arm is related to the muscular, hydraulic, mechanical, etc.

What is more, it is only on a certain supposition that the relation between normative and neural explanations of action is relevantly similar to the homeostasis model at all. This is the supposition that the action just *is* the bodily movement (no doubt suitably attended by appropriate causes), at least for every case in which action 'involves' bodily movement. This gives us, or would give us, that the neural explanation explains the very same thing as does the reasons-explanation, which is what we are looking for. But, sadly, it is also very implausible, as we see once we distinguish in the now standard way between two senses of 'bodily movement', the first being what we might call a 'movedness' of the body, something suitably preceded by and caused by some neural disturbances, and the second being a moving of the body, conceived as something done by an agent. With this distinction in hand matters now divide up, the neural explanation attaching itself to how it gets to happen that the hand rises, how it works, while the reasons-explanation concerns itself with why the owner of the hand raises it. Of course the two explanations are not thereby completely torn apart, but the question of the relation between them becomes that of the relation between the movedness and the moving—between what it is tempting to think of as a mere event and what looks much more like an action that 'involves' such an event. The matter begins to depend, that is, on whatever we think we mean by 'involving' in this case. And however we resolve that issue, it seems that once we have ceased to presume that the action is identical with the event involved, we can no longer say that the neural explanation is an account of how the action 'works'. All we can say is that there is an account of how the movement involved works, which is not at all what we wanted. The causal explanation, therefore, turns out not to be in competition with the reasons-explanation; but this has not emerged quite in the way that we had hoped, for we have not ended up with two explanations of the same thing. (In particular, there is nothing here that yet threatens the advocates of human freedom.)

If we want a systematic relation between reasons-explanations and causal explanations, therefore, we are going to have to look elsewhere. The only remaining possibility seems to me to be a causal explanation of the agent's acting for the reason that he did, i.e. a causal explanation within which normative considerations have been subsumed as a feature of that which is to be explained. That explanation might itself be in a broader sense psychological. Kant uses this term to refer to the sorts of empirical explanation of action that he is willing to countenance. Such explanations appeal, not to the agent's current beliefs and desires, but to things like the agent's dispositions, character, background, and upbringing.[7] Of the perpetrator of a malicious lie, Kant suggests that for an empirical explanation we look to 'defective education, bad company . . . the viciousness of a natural disposition insensitive to shame . . . levity and thoughtlessness' (1781, A554/B582).

We need not here get hung up about the distinction between event and action. No matter how vigorously we might want to distinguish actions from events, that the action was done for those reasons is here to be considered as an event, something that happens, not itself something that was done by someone. So we could take ourselves to be dealing with nested explanations, the normative one being placed within a causal one. In every case where we run an explanation of the normative sort, there will presumably be a possible further question how it was that the agent was the sort of person to be influenced by such features. In a case where the features that the agent was influenced by were the right ones, we are unlikely to raise this further question. But it could still

---

[7] I take it that Kant is suspicious of what would nowadays be thought of as the standard explanation of action in terms of beliefs of the agent, since he would think of it as a misreading of the rational explanation in terms of the agent's response to reasons.

be raised, and if it is, the answer to it is likely to be in terms of the agent's upbringing or his settled nature, or something like that. (We could think of this as an Aristotelian explanation of the acquisition of a virtue.) But in another case we might explain his not coming to the party, first by laying out the considerations in the light of which he decided not to come, and second by supporting this first explanation by explaining how he could have been persuaded by such a thing to stay away. Perhaps he is just embarrassingly shy. Here we appeal to a psychological state of the agent to explain, and defend, our normative-style explanation of his choice. But this does nothing to show that the explanation of action is not as the normative story has it. Explanation is surely always nested, or at least nestable, in this way. Each answer to a demand for explanation raises a further potential explanatory question. In the causal case, for instance, if I specify C as the cause of E, one may ask how it could come about that C was capable of causing E. This may be thought of as a further causal question, so that the nesting of explanations here is a causal nesting. But there is no need in general for the nesting to be homogeneous. If the nested explanation is causal, for instance, that in which it is nested might well appeal, not to further events as causes, but to causal laws, which cannot themselves be causes at all. So I take it that there can be (indeed, may always be) an explanation of the success of a particular normative explanation that involves appeal to psychological states of the agent (or other matters of a non-normative sort), without this doing anything to show that normative explanation is itself a covert form of psychologistic explanation, or in general something other than what it purports to be.[8]

---

[8] This matter is relevant to the ability of the normative story to accommodate what is normally called weakness of will, the oddity of which lies in the agent's ability to act *despite* judging that the balance of reasons favours something else. We can, none the less, lay out the light in which the agent saw the action, and appeal to that to explain why he did what he did. We will have been forced, that is, to distinguish two things that I have commonly run together, the favourable light in which the agent saw the action and the light in which he saw the situation. What explains his doing what he did is the former light. What should, but in the present case does not, explain his doing this rather than anything else is the relation between the former and the latter light. My own view is that when we are dealing with a case of weakness of will, explanation of this comparative sort is stymied. This, I take it, is a defect common to all theories of action-explanation that are, as one might put it, rationalistic. The relevant comparative explanation will not be rationalistic, therefore, but will probably be psychological in some way.

This might give us the sort of accommodation between the claims of causal and non-causal explanation that we have been seeking. Indeed, it may now seem that we have in place the materials for separating the three styles of explanation that we have considered in such a way that they are quite incapable of conflicting, since each is in the business of answering its own question and is quite unconcerned with the questions that engross the other two. The action, we have said, is not the movement. There is, however, a question how the movement works, and the neural explanation is addressed to this. There is the question what were the considerations in the light of which the agent chose to do what he did, and the normative explanation is addressed to this. Then there is the question how it came about that these reasons appealed to him, and this we answer by talking of his education, experience, upbringing, etc. If these are just three quite different questions, there is no danger of any of the answers to them getting in the way of each other.

There are undeniable attractions in this 'divide and rule' approach. But yet I think that we should not in the end be satisfied with it—or at least, not yet. First, it is true that we have distinguished between action and movement. But we have no clear idea of the 'involving' relation that ties the action to the movement. And we should not be trying to think of the action as another object like the movement, though not identical with it. This whole issue is obscure, and that fact alone should make us hesitate to announce that *just* because the action is not the movement, there can be no question of 'how the action works' in the way that there is a question 'how the movement works'. We should remember that our argument on the point was merely epistemological. We did not say 'Since this is the case, the action is not the movement'. We said 'Since we do not understand this issue, we cannot say that the action is the movement'. Second, the idea that the normative explanation will always be nested within a causal one needs further defence. For even if the object whose explanation we are seeking (the action being done for those reasons) is to be taken as an event, its explanation may often be normative. We may, that is, often explain such a thing by pointing out that the reasons concerned were extremely cogent and pressing ones, i.e. by offering more in the way of the normative, not by resorting to a causal explanation of the normative relation already in place. (Causal explanations, as always, are more attractive when things go wrong than when they go right.) If we ask how he came to act for these reasons, our answer may start by pointing out that they were very good reasons. We may continue, perhaps, by alluding to his fine upbringing. But in doing so we appear to be adding this causal explanation to a normative one, and nothing in the divide and rule approach of the previous paragraph has shown us how to do this.

But despite all this, if our question is merely whether the sort of causal explanation that appeals to character, upbringing, *et al.* is compatible with a normative explanation of the action itself in terms of the reasons in the light of which the agent acted, the answer appears here to be an unproblematic yes. Consider again the example of being sent to prison for having committed a crime rather than for having been convicted, discussed at the end of Chapter 6; even if one's having been committed is not part of the normative explanation of why one was sent to prison, it is part of the causal story of one's ending up there none the less. This sort of possibility is instructive, for it gives us a different model of a way in which two distinct explanations can combine. There surely is no mystery about how an action can be *partly* explained in normative terms and *partly* explained in 'upbringing' terms. We should allow this as a possibility, even after we have abandoned as fragile the 'divide and rule' policy that thinks of the two explanations as addressing quite different questions.

It is worth noting, however, why one particular version of the strategy suggested in the preceding paragraph will not work. This version maintains that the psychologistic explanation in terms of the beliefs of the agent is exactly the causal explanation of the agent's having acted for the reason that he did. He acted for the reason that he did because he had certain beliefs that led him so to act. This may be viewed as the last resort of the psychologist. But it must fail—or at least it is incompatible with the normative story. For that story allots to the agent's believing as he did a certain role, namely that of a necessary or enabling condition. And an enabling condition for an explanation cannot be converted into an explanation of things being as the first explanation has it. The success of the first explanation requires the presence of the necessary condition, which, were it then also to play the role of an explanation of that success, would be partly in the business of explaining itself.

The real problem, then, comes when one tries to understand the possible relations between normative explanation of action and neural explanations of movement. The final spasms of a book whose main focus is elsewhere is not the place to address this enormous issue, sadly—or perhaps not so sadly, since at this point we are getting close to the topic of human freedom, to which glib answers are never going to be welcome. The only contribution that this book attempts to make to the issue is to recast it. The question is no longer one about the relation between two causal explanations of action, the first given in terms of psychological states of the agent, the second in terms of neural states of the agent. It is now about the relation between a causal explanation of a bodily movement conceived as an event, run in terms of neural changes and states, on one side, and a non-causal explanation of action in terms of supposedly good reasons. It seems to me that this change makes a difference to the problem by altering what could count as a resolution to it. For instance, it obviously means that no subtle suggestions from within the philosophy of mind about the relation between psychological states and states of the brain is going to generate the sort of resolution that is required. I do not suppose, however, that the now recast problem can be solved without appeal to considerations that take us far beyond what we have already achieved.

BIBLIOGRAPHY

ALTHAM, J. E. J., and HARRISON, R. (eds.) (1995), *World, Mind and Ethics: Essays on the Ethical Philosophy of Bernard Williams* (Cambridge: Cambridge University Press).

ANSCOMBE, G. E. M. (1957), *Intention* (Oxford: Blackwell).

—— (1989), 'Von Wright on Practical Inference', in P. A. Schilpp (ed.), *The Philosophy of Georg Henrik von Wright* (LaSalle, Ill.: Open Court); repr. as 'Practical Inference', in Hursthouse *et al.* (1995: 1–34).

BAIER, K. (1958), *The Moral Point of View* (Ithaca, NY: Cornell University Press).

BERGSTRÖM, L. (1996), 'Reflections on Consequentialism', *Theoria*, 62/1–2: 74–94.

BOND, E. J. (1983), *Reason and Value* (Cambridge: Cambridge University Press).

BRINK, D. O. (1989), *Moral Realism and the Foundations of Ethics* (Cambridge: Cambridge University Press).

BROOME, J. (1997), 'Reasons and Motivation', *Proceedings of the Aristotelian Society*, suppl. vol. 71: 131–46.

—— (1999), 'Normative Requirements', *Ratio*, 12/3: 398–419; repr. in Dancy (2000c: 78–99).

—— (forthcoming), 'Practical Reasoning'.

CHANG, R. (ed.) (1998), *Incommensurability, Incomparability and Practical Reason* (Cambridge, Mass.: Harvard University Press).

CHILD, W. (1994), *Causality, Interpretation, and the Mind* (Oxford: Clarendon Press).

CHISHOLM, R. M. (1963), 'Contrary-to-Duty Imperatives and Deontic Logic', *Analysis*, 34/2: 33–6.

COLLINS, A. W. (1984), 'Action, Causality and Teleological Explanation', in P. A. French *et al.* (eds.), *Midwest Studies in Philosophy*, ix: *Causation and Causal Theories* (Notre Dame, Ind.: University of Notre Dame Press), 344–69; reworked as ch. 6 of Collins (1987: 120–51).

—— (1987), *The Nature of Mental Things* (Notre Dame, Ind.: University of Notre Dame Press).

—— (1997), 'The Psychological Reality of Reasons', *Ratio*, 10/2: 108–23.

CRISP, R. (1996), 'The Dualism of Practical Reason', *Proceedings of the Aristotelian Society*, 96: 53–73.

—— and HOOKER, B. W. (eds.) (2000), *Well-Being and Morality: Essays in Honour of James Griffin* (Oxford: Oxford University Press).

CULLITY, G., and GAUT, B. (eds.) (1997), *Ethics and Practical Reason* (Oxford: Clarendon Press).

DANCY, J. (1977), 'The Logical Conscience', *Analysis*, 37/2: 81–4.

——(1993), *Moral Reasons* (Oxford: Blackwell).

——(1995*a*), 'Why there is Really no such Thing as the Theory of Motivation', *Proceedings of the Aristotelian Society*, 95: 1–18.

——(1995*b*), 'Arguments from Illusion', *Philosophical Quarterly*, 45/181: 421–38.

——(1996), 'Real Values in a Humean Context', *Ratio*, 9/2: 171–83.

——(ed.) (1997), *Reading Parfit* (Oxford: Blackwell).

——(2000*a*), 'Recognition and Reaction', in Crisp and Hooker (2000).

——(2000*b*), 'Should we Pass the Buck?', in A. O'Hear (ed.), *The Good, the True and the Beautiful* (Cambridge: Cambridge University Press), 159–73.

——(ed.) (2000*c*), *Normativity* (Oxford: Blackwell).

——(2001), 'Prichard on Duty and Ignorance of Fact', in P. J. Stratton-Lake (ed.), *Ethical Intuitionism: Re-evaluations* (Oxford: Oxford University Press).

DARWALL, S. (1983), *Impartial Reason* (Ithaca, NY: Cornell University Press).

DAVIDSON, D. (1980), *Essays on Actions and Events* (Oxford: Oxford University Press).

EDGLEY, R. (1969), *Reason in Theory and Practice* (London: Hutchinson University Library).

FALK, W. D. (1947–8), ' "Ought" and Motivation', *Proceedings of the Aristotelian Society*, 48: 492–510; repr. in Falk (1986: 21–41).

——(1986), *Ought, Reasons, and Morality* (Ithaca, NY: Cornell University Press).

FOOT, P. (1995), 'Does Moral Subjectivism Rest on a Mistake?', *Oxford Journal of Legal Studies*, 15/1: 1–14.

FRANKENA, W. K. (1958), 'Obligation and Motivation', in Melden (1958: 40–81).

GARRARD, E., and MCNAUGHTON, D. (1998), 'Mapping Moral Motivation', *Ethical Theory and Moral Practice*, 1: 45–59.

GREENSPAN, P. (1975), 'Conditional Oughts and Hypothetical Imperatives', *Journal of Philosophy*, 72/10: 259–76.

GRICE, G. R. (1967), *The Grounds of Moral Judgement* (Cambridge: Cambridge University Press).

HACKER, P. M. S. (1992), 'Malcolm and Searle on "Intentional Mental States" ', *Philosophical Investigations*, 15/3: 245–75.

HEIL, J., and MELE, A. (eds.) (1995), *Mental Causation* (Oxford: Oxford University Press).

HORNSBY, J. (1995), 'Agency and Mental Causation', in Heil and Mele

Bibliography   181

(1995: 161–88); repr. as ch. 8 of her *Simple Mindedness* (Cambridge, Mass.: Harvard University Press, 1997), 129–53.

HUMBERSTONE, L. (1992), 'Direction of Fit', *Mind*, 101: 59–83.

HUME, D. (1739–40), *A Treatise of Human Nature*, ed. P. Nidditch (Oxford: Oxford University Press, 1978).

HUNTER, J. (1980), 'Believing', in P. A. French *et al.* (eds.), *Midwest Studies in Philosophy*, v: *Epistemology* (Notre Dame, Ind.: University of Notre Dame Press), 239–60.

HURSTHOUSE, R., LAWRENCE, G., and QUINN, W. (eds.) (1995), *Virtues and Reasons* (Oxford: Clarendon Press).

HUTCHESON, F. (1728), *Illustrations upon the Moral Sense*, sect. 1; repr. abridged in L. A. Selby-Bigge (ed.), *British Moralists*, 2 vols. (Oxford: Clarendon Press, 1897), i. 403–18.

KANT, I. (1781), *Critique of Pure Reason*; trans. N. Kemp Smith (London: Macmillan, 1961).

KORSGAARD, C. M. (1986), 'Scepticism about Practical Reason', *Journal of Philosophy*, 83: 5–25; repr. in Korsgaard (1996: 311–34).

—— (1996), *Creating the Kingdom of Ends* (Cambridge: Cambridge University Press).

—— (1997), 'The Normativity of Instrumental Reason', in Cullity and Gaut (1997: 215–54).

McDOWELL, J. (1978), 'Are Moral Requirements Hypothetical Imperatives?', *Proceedings of the Aristotelian Society*, suppl. vol. 52: 13–29.

—— (1979), 'Virtue and Reason', *Monist*, 62: 331–50.

—— (1985), 'Functionalism and Anomalous Monism', in E. LePore and B. McLaughlin (eds.), *Actions and Events: Perspectives on the Philosophy of Donald Davidson* (Oxford: Blackwell), 386–98.

—— (1994), *Mind and World* (Cambridge, Mass.: Harvard University Press).

—— (1995), 'Are there External Reasons?', in Altham and Harrison (1995: 68–85).

MALCOLM, N. (1968), 'The Conceivability of Mechanism', *Philosophical Review*, 77: 45–72.

—— (1991), ' "I believe that *p* " ', in E. Lepore and R. van Gulick (eds.), *John Searle and his Critics* (Oxford: Blackwell), 159–67.

MARTIN, M. G. F. (1997), 'The Reality of Appearances', in M. Sainsbury (ed.), *Thought and Ontology* (Milan: F. Angeli), 81–106.

MELDEN, A. I. (ed.) (1958), *Essays in Moral Philosophy* (Seattle: University of Washington Press).

MELLOR, D. H. (1995), *The Facts of Causation* (London: Routledge).

MOORE, G. E. (1903), *Principia Ethica* (Cambridge: Cambridge University Press).

MOORE, G. E. (1912), *Ethics* (Cambridge: Cambridge University Press).

NAGEL, T. (1970), *The Possibility of Altruism* (Princeton: Princeton University Press).

——(1986), *The View from Nowhere* (Oxford: Oxford University Press).

PARFIT, D. (1984), *Reasons and Persons* (Oxford: Oxford University Press).

——(1997), 'Reasons and Motivation', *Proceedings of the Aristotelian Society*, suppl. vol. 71: 99–130.

PETTIT, P., and SMITH, M. (1990), 'Backgrounding Desire', *Philosophical Review*, 99: 564–92.

————(1997), 'Parfit's P', in Dancy (1997: 71–95).

PLANTINGA, A. (1974), *The Nature of Necessity* (Oxford: Clarendon Press).

PRICHARD, H. A. (1912), 'Does Moral Philosophy Rest on a Mistake?', *Mind*, 21: 21–37; repr. in Prichard (1949: 1–17).

——(1932), 'Duty and Ignorance of Fact', in Prichard (1949: 18–39).

——(1949), *Moral Obligation*, ed. W. D. Ross (Oxford: Clarendon Press).

QUINN, W. (1992), 'Rationality and the Human Good', *Social Philosophy and Policy*, 9/2: 81–95; repr. in Quinn (1993*b*: 210–27).

——(1993*a*), 'Putting Rationality in its Place', in R. Frey and C. Morris (eds.), *Value, Welfare and Morality* (Cambridge: Cambridge University Press); repr. in Quinn (1993*b*: 228–55) and in Hursthouse *et al.* (1995: 181–208).

——(1993*b*), *Morality and Action* (Cambridge: Cambridge University Press).

RABINOWICZ, W., and OSTERBERG, J. (1996), 'Value-Based Preferences: On Two Interpretations of Preference Utilitarianism', *Economics and Philosophy*, 12: 1–27.

RAPOPORT, J. L. (1989), *The Boy who Couldn't Stop Washing: The Experience and Treatment of Obsessive-Compulsive Disorder* (New York: Penguin Books).

RAZ, J. (ed.) (1978), *Practical Reason* (Oxford: Oxford University Press).

——(1986), *The Morality of Freedom* (Oxford: Clarendon Press).

——(1994), *Ethics in the Public Domain* (Oxford: Clarendon Press).

——(1998), 'Incommensurability and Agency', in Chang (1998: 110–28).

REGAN, D. (1980), *Utilitarianism and Co-operation* (Oxford: Clarendon Press).

ROBINSON, W. S. (1990), 'States and Beliefs', *Mind*, 99/393: 33–51.

ROSS, W. D. (1930), *The Right and the Good* (Oxford: Clarendon Press).

——(1939), *Foundations of Ethics* (Oxford: Clarendon Press).

RUNDLE, B. (1997), *Mind in Action* (Oxford: Clarendon Press).

SCANLON, T. (1999), *What we Owe to Each Other* (Cambridge, Mass.: Harvard University Press).

SCHUELER, G. F. (1995), *Desire: Its Role in Practical Reason and the Explanation of Action* (Cambridge, Mass.: MIT Press).

Bibliography

SEARLE, J. (1983), *Intentionality* (Cambridge: Cambridge University Press).

SELBY-BIGGE, L. A. (ed.) (1897), *British Moralists*, 2 vols. (Oxford: Clarendon Press).

SKORUPSKI, J. (1997), 'Reasons and Reason', in Cullity and Gaut (1997: 345–68).

SMITH, M. (1987), 'The Humean Theory of Motivation', *Mind*, 96: 36–61.

——(1994), *The Moral Problem* (Oxford: Blackwell).

STALNAKER, R. (1984), *Inquiry* (Cambridge, Mass.: MIT Press).

STAMPE, D. W. (1987), 'The Authority of Desire', *Philosophical Review*, 96/3: 335–81.

STEWARD, H. (1997), *The Ontology of Mind* (Oxford: Clarendon Press).

STOUT, R. (1996), *Things that Happen because they Should* (Oxford: Oxford University Press).

STOUTLAND, F. (1976), 'The Causation of Behaviour', in *Essays on Wittgenstein in Honour of G. H. von Wright*, Acta Philosophica Fennica, 28: 286–325.

——(1986), 'Reasons, Causes and Intentional Explanation', *Analyse & Kritik*, 8: 28–55.

——(1998), 'The Real Reasons', in J. Bransen and S. E. Cuypers (eds.), *Human Action, Deliberation and Causation* (Dordrecht: Kluwer Academic Publishers), 43–66.

——(1999), 'Intentionalists and Davidson on Rational Explanation', in G. Meggle (ed.), *Actions, Norms, Values* (Berlin: Walter de Gruyter), 191–208.

TAYLOR, C. (1964), *The Explanation of Behaviour* (London: Routledge & Kegan Paul).

VENDLER, Z. (1962), 'Effects, Results and Consequences', in R. J. Butler (ed.), *Analytic Philosophy* (Oxford: Blackwell), 1–14.

——(1967), 'Causal Relations', *Journal of Philosophy*, 64: 704–13.

WALLACE, R. J. (1990), 'How to Argue about Practical Reason', *Mind*, 99: 355–85.

WATSON, G. (1975), 'Free Agency', *Journal of Philosophy*, 72/8: 205–20; repr. in G. Watson (ed.), *Free Will* (Oxford: Oxford University Press, 1982), 96–110.

WHITE, A. R. (1972), 'What we Believe', in N. Rescher (ed.), *Studies in the Philosophy of Mind*, APQ monograph series no. 6 (Oxford: Blackwell), 69–84.

WIGGINS, D. (1975–6), 'Deliberation and Practical Reason', *Proceedings of the Aristotelian Society*, 76: 29–51; repr. in Wiggins (1987: 215–37).

——(1987), *Needs, Values, Truth: Essays in the Philosophy of Value* (Oxford: Blackwell).

——(1995), 'Categorical Requirements: Hume and Kant on the Idea of Duty', in Hursthouse *et al.* (1995: 297–330).

WILLIAMS, B. A. O. (1980), 'Internal and External Reasons', in R. Harrison (ed.), *Rational Action* (Cambridge: Cambridge University Press), 17–28; repr. in Williams (1981: 101–13).

——(1981), *Moral Luck* (Cambridge: Cambridge University Press).

——(1989), 'Internal Reasons and the Obscurity of Blame', *Logos*, 10: 1–12; repr. in Williams (1995: 35–45).

WILLIAMS, B. A. O. (1995), *Making Sense of Humanity* (Cambridge: Cambridge University Press).

WOODS, M. (1972), 'Reasons for Action and Desire', *Proceedings of the Aristotelian Society*, suppl. vol. 46: 189–201.

WRIGHT, G. H. von (1980), *Freedom and Determination*, Acta Philosophica Fennica, 31/1.

WRIGHT, L. (1976), *Teleological Explanation* (Berkeley: University of California Press).

INDEX

vs. motives 22, 23
objective vs. subjective 49–52, 60–1,
    105; *see also* objectivity
opposing 4–5
theoretical 105, 146
reasons (motivating):
    acting for a reason that is no reason
        2, 3–4, 141–2, 144
    good motivating reasons 118–19
    as motivating states 14–15; *see also*
        psychologism
    see also Humeanism, psychologism
reasons (normative):
    agent-centred vs. agent-neutral 17n
    desire-based vs. value-based 17–19;
        see also desire-based reasons
    'my normative reasons' 7
    need agents 155
    normative nature of 1, 26–7, 29
    not knowing as a reason 56, 58, 69
    not propositions 114–17
    propositional 121–2
    reasons vs. rationality 60
    and thin properties 150
    value-based vs. content-based 29–30
reasons-why 5–6
Regan, T. 57
Ross, W. D. 11, 72n

Scanlon, T. 30n, 35, 39, 88, 115
Schueler, G. F. 80, 93n
Simple Argument 32–3
Smith, M. 7, 8–10, 78n, 91
sound deliberative route 15–16, 27n
Stalnaker, R. 115n
Steward, H. 123n, 159n, 160–1
Stout, R. 139n
Stoutland, F. 165n

three-part story 100–13; *see also*
    psychologism
tie-breakers 39–40
transference rules 66–8
triangulation argument 151–3

urges 36

Vendler, Z. 159n

Wallace, R. J. 118n
Watson, G. 35n
weakness of will 174n
White, A. R. 147–8
Williams, B. A. O. 15–17, 18, 26–9, 121,
    151–8
Wingrave, Owen (example) 155–6
Wright, L. 165